Published by LONGSTREET PRESS, INC.,
a subsidiary of Cox Newspapers,
a subsidiary of Cox Enterprises, Inc.
2140 Newmarket Parkway
Suite 118
Marietta, Georgia 30067

Printed in the United States of America

1st printing, 1996

Library of Congress Catalog Number 95-82240

ISBN: 1-56352-287-X

This book was printed in the United States

Jacket/Book design by Neil Hollingsworth

Digital film prep and separations by Advertising Technologies, Inc., Atlanta, GA

WE DANCE BECAUSE WE CAN
PEOPLE OF THE POWWOW

✳

Photography by
DON CONTRERAS

Text by
DIANE MORRIS BERNSTEIN

To the memory of
MICHAEL ORR
(1971-1993)

To my wife,
RHONDA,
for her infinite love and patience
—D.C.

To my children,
CHASE and **GABRIELLE,**
who I hope will carry on the traditions of our people
—D.M.B.

TABLE OF CONTENTS

Foreword

For over three and a half years we have been traveling the back roads, the dirt roads, the steep mountain roads to powwows. When we began our journey, we knew very little about Native Americans. We had read history books in school, seen movies as kids, heard various stories over the years, but neither of us had actually met these people or talked with them.

Our quest for the people of the powwow began with a photograph. It then developed into an idea for a book about dance and regalia. But after a few interviews, we realized that the book needed to be more; it needed to be their thoughts expressed in their words.

Admittedly, our initial efforts were difficult. After all, there had been more than enough journalists, writers, historians, and photographers who had taken these people's words and images and distorted or misused them for personal gain. So, naturally at first, they were hesitant to talk to us. Once we proved that we sincerely wished to understand and respect their traditions, it was amazing how quickly word traveled the powwow circuit, and the book took on a life of its own.

Powwows are for all people—young and old. They are exciting intertribal gatherings with dancers and drums, who represent many nations with their regalia, dance, and music; crafts-people, who provide beautiful handmade objects fashioned in traditional and contemporary styles; and vendors, who provide the flavors of the Native American kitchen.

We have learned a lot about these people, their ways and traditions. We have learned many personal lessons, too: like not to take the history we read in books as children, even as adults, at face value. Talking with members of the different tribes, we have gotten a small but important glimpse of the unwritten history, a history that comes from an oral tradition, a history told from the other point of view.

Perhaps one of the most important things we have learned is that Native Americans are a wonderful, hospitable people. They care about their people, about other people, and about Mother Earth. We are grateful for the friendships we have made along the way. We could not have put this book together without the help and guidance of Diamond Brown, Bobbie Orr, and Chipa Wolf, who introduced us to their people, to their friends, and to other tribes.

We were enriched by this experience; our eyes were opened. By no means do we believe that we are now experts on Native Americans. We have only begun our quest for knowledge; learning is a lifelong pursuit.

We hope that, if nothing else, this book will encourage people to attend a powwow, to have an open mind, to throw away the stereotypes, and to really listen to these people, to what they have to say. They have an important story to tell.

Diane Morris Bernstein
Don Contreras

WE DANCE BECAUSE WE CAN
PEOPLE OF THE POWWOW

CLINT CAYOU
OMAHA PONCA LAKOTA WINNEBAGO

"WE DANCE BECAUSE WE CAN."

At every powwow there is at least one dancer whose presence can be felt, can be sensed before he enters the circle. Clint Cayou is such a dancer. He exudes the self-confidence and power of a warrior in his every movement, his every gesture; yet, his soft, melodic voice and kindly manner reveal the gentleness that is within. He knows his people. He knows himself. He speaks with wisdom beyond his years.

"I am Omaha Ponca Lakota Winnebago. Omaha Bird Clan. We are the sky people. So when we dance that's how we act. We act like something from the sky—soaring birds or attacking birds."

Clint is deliberate in describing his regalia, careful to express its meaning and significance. "All of the leather I made myself. These bones here (epaulets), these are deer hooves. My grandmother is Deer Clan, so in honor of her I wear these. My moccasins are leather rawhide. My roach [headpiece] is deer tail and porcupine guard hair. These circles, medicine wheels, these are the four directions. It's round; everything that's in power is a circle.

You look at a bird's nest, it's round. You look at a tree and it's round. Look at our bodies, they are round. The world is round. We knew that a long, long time ago; we never ever thought it was flat. We knew those things, everyday knowledge.

"These abalone shells are for decoration. My shield is black. This is the tail feathers of a rough-legged hawk and its white face. A friend of mine gave this to me. It came all the way from Montana. I made this fan. I don't think you'll see any like it anywhere. It has left and right wing spikes of an eagle so I can carry it in either hand. Usually the right side is reserved for men and the left side for women, but I decided to use it my own way. It is my interpretation of a fan.

"This dance stick is a horse. There is a hoof at one end and a face at the other. If you notice, he's carrying me. He's a representation of something I had at one time. To honor that horse, I carry this stick. These feathers [on the dance stick] are crow feathers. I honor the crow because they fight owls. Owls bring bad things, bad people, bad news, death. Crows, they fight owls, so we honor them.

black lines represent the powers of the West, for dealing out death to scare my enemies, to intimidate my enemies. I've had this pattern since I was 11 years old. I'm 32 now, so it's been 21 years and it's always been the same. That way, God will recognize me. God will see who I am and take me in. I think that the difference between us and most non-Indians is that we don't believe in hell. We have no hell. God loves us. Otherwise, why would he give us so many different kinds of trees, so many different kinds of plants and all these fish and animals to eat, and all the different people? Why would he give us all that? God loves us; he's going to say, 'Come here, you messed up. Quit it.' We'll know what we did wrong."

Clint dances Men's Northern Traditional. "This dance is very old. This dance is older than Jesus, way older. This is the Omaha Wachega Helushka, the Omaha warrior dance, and we started it. People came and they saw it, and they said, 'We like that dance.' We said, 'Be our friends and have this dance. We give it to you, we share it with you.' So now it's all over Canada, all over the U.S., in Georgia, Montana, California, Florida. Not everybody knows why they are doing it, but they're doing it. It's a dance for celebration, a dance for life. It's a dance for the changing of the seasons.

"That circle [pointing to the dance circle], it's sacred. They bless it. They pray for it. When you go out there you have to keep yourself in a holy manner. Keep yourself where you're thinking about what you're doing, you're enjoying yourself. Sometimes you can just let go and be all right. I've been around the arena since I was too small to walk. It's [the dance] there, you don't have to pass it on. It's there, it's ours. We have the right to do that. We dance because we can. We dance hard because we can. Omaha dancers, we dance hard because it's our dance. We're dancing for old people, we're dancing for young ones. They are out there, so you have to be strong for them. I was raised by my grandparents. What they had they gave to me to bring me up right — to try to be fair, to try to be equal, try to be generous, try to be good. Anymore, though, it's hard. A lot of people, they mistake kindness for weakness. You got to know what you're doing when you get out there. You can't get out there and just move around, it doesn't count. It may be okay, but it doesn't count.

"If my wife is at home sick, I don't pray just for her, I don't pray for myself. I ask for strength to find an answer. Then I pray for everybody, the whole world — these trees,

These eagle feathers, there's great power in these. These are cut a certain way here to represent certain things my family has done. My dad, my grandfather, and my uncles and I dance for all of them. I dance for all those people when I dance. I dance for old people. I dance for little ones. I dance for my family. I dance for my grandmother. I dance for my dad. He was in Vietnam."

One of Clint's most striking features is his face paint. Not all dancers, in fact very few, wear face paint. "Amongst my Omaha people we have different colors that are power colors, passion colors, protection colors. The black on my lips is going to keep evil from entering into my body. It's going to repel that evil. The white is the strength of the North. It bowls my enemies over. The

War shield

this grass, all these people here. That's one thing I think other people should do, try to remember the little ones who are sick, not just their little ones that are sick, but all the little ones that are sick. Got no place to go, got no place to wash up, got no place to eat. That's one thing we try to do, try to keep in mind that we are not the only ones here. Always try your best. If you don't try your best you're cheatin' yourself, and if you don't tell the truth you're hurtin' something out there. If you hurt something, you can't take it back."

BOBBIE ORR
SALISH

"WE ARE A PROUD PEOPLE.
WE ARE A RACE OF SURVIVORS; WE HAVE TO BE."

Bobbie Orr is a quiet, sensitive woman with a wonderful sense of humor. She is a member of the Confederated Salish and Kootenai tribes of the Flathead Reservation in the northwest corner of Montana. "Most of my life, from the time I was nine years old until I graduated from school, I was raised by a white family. Our house burned down; and, rather than placing us with relatives where we would be able to continue to learn about our people, they placed Indian children with white families. I didn't really learn anything [about Indian ways] until my son was born in 1971. I always had an interest in things, and I always knew I was Indian because I was raised on the reservation."

Watching Bobbie Orr dance is like seeing a field of wheat blowing in a gentle breeze. Her movements are slow, light, and precise, barely perceptible if not for the softly swaying fringe of her buckskin dress. "I am a Traditional Buckskin Dancer. The Traditional Buckskin is a very graceful, slow moving dance. It took a while to get the money to make my dress, so I didn't start dancing

until 1990. You have thousands of dollars in these dresses, and I'm still working on mine. The more bead-work you add to it, well, it's a never-ending job.

"My dress is patterned after my grandmother's dress. I have a picture that was taken when she was in her twenties. When she died, her dress was taken by her white sisters-in-law who wouldn't have anything to do with her [while she was living] because they disowned their brother when he married an Indian woman. But once she died, they stepped in and took all her Indian regalia, her dress, her moccasins, everything that was the old beaded style.

"We found out just two years ago that the dress is in a museum somewhere in Montana or Canada. And that particular beaded pattern, the only time I have ever seen it is on my grandmother's dress. The Salish people combine the floral pattern and the geometric pattern; they are one of the few tribes that combine both patterns. It looks like a heart made into a flower. The long fringe on the front of the dress is very unusual. It makes it just a little bit different — a little bit more Salish in style.

"When I made my dress I had a picture of my grandmother, and I just tried to follow it as closely as I could. All my mother could remember was that the colors were your basic reds, yellows, blues, whites. I had to guess at how it was put together. I've done all the beadwork myself. So to me, when I dance, I dance for my grandmother. It is honoring her.

"When I dance, I have a redtail hawk feather that I wear, and I also carry a hawk fan. I wear an eagle feather on the top of my head. That is my veteran's feather. I am a Women's Army Corps veteran. My brother did two tours of duty over in Vietnam; my father and six of his seven brothers were all in the military. So to me, the veteran feather covers everyone in the family."

The Bitterroot Valley was the ancestral home of the Salish people. In 1855 they signed the Hellgate Treaty, which was supposed to remove them to the Flathead Valley. "Our chief, Chief Victor, refused to move his people for 20 years after this treaty was signed because the Bitterroot Valley was our ancestral home. Every year there is a pilgrimage back to the Bitterroot Valley to gather the bitterroot, a medicine plant used in the ceremonies. One time, in order to keep the tribal members from going back there, the white people poisoned the bitterroot plants.

"I was born in Mission Valley; my son was born there, my grandmothers, mother, father. We are called the Salish Flathead. The name Flathead was given to the Salish by mistake. The white man mistakenly thought we were a Pacific Coast tribe who really do flatten their babies' heads. They consider it a sign of beauty. But, to us, we are the Salish.

"We are on one side of the Flathead Reservation, and the Kootenai are on the other side. They were actually more our enemies at the time, but, of course, the government put us together on one reservation. Most of the time, we do get along very well. We are a lucky people because of our reservation of 1.2 million acres. Over half of it, however, is owned by white people, because as soon as they made the reservation and set up the treaty rights, they realized that it was very rich land agriculturally. So, all of a sudden, you have all these white people that want the land.

"The Dixon Act opened it up for settlement. They considered it surplus land if we didn't use it, which meant they went in and got the best agricultural land on the reservation. Each year our tribe sets aside money to buy back land. Hopefully, someday, we can own it all again.

It might be a long time away. We also control the water rights, after a long court battle, so we can regulate the rivers and the lakes. A lot of time the white farmers would run a creek dry just so they could water their crops. It was like they didn't care that there would be no water next year or that the fish would die; all they wanted was their full crop. In the past few years we have started regulating it and started reverting those streams back to their natural state rather than make them reservoirs to bring water to farmers.

"In 1977 we established a Salish Kootenai College on the reservation, and it is one of the better Indian colleges in the U.S. White people go to it also. It is a two-year college. We just opened a resort and convention center. A lot of this takes money back to the tribe. We get what we call per capita payments — from money the tribe has made. Three times a year they send us a certain percentage of the tribal income. Also, part of that goes into education and other developments on the reservation. But they set aside certain money that will always go back to the members.

"In that part of Montana you couldn't have gotten bad land. The tribe has learned how to come to terms with the white man's world. We know that we have to invest. We know that we have to establish things. We still have our problems — drugs, the suicide rate, alcohol. Everybody has those problems. We have learned for quite some time now to stand on our own two feet. We are a strong tribe.

"The Salish have been in that area for many years. Like a lot of tribes, you learn the white ways to survive. Back about 20 years ago, they just started teaching the language again in the schools. The Salish Kootenai College teaches it. We have kept up our ceremonies; we have kept up our dances. So we are still a proud people. We are a race of survivors; we have to be. Because even today, our worst enemy is still the American government. They still want to run us out, make us mainstream. The Indian people don't want to be like everyone else."

Bobbie and her son, Michael, still carry on the traditional ways of the Salish people. "I am very proud that my son was able to go to a Salish sweat. I told him to learn from it. The sweat lodge is the lodge we go in to pray. It is Mother Earth's womb. So, when we sit in there and we bring in the rocks and add the water that is lifegiver to those rocks, to me that is the one place

Jerry Ward and Bobby Orr

I can always find peace. I don't go to a church, but when I'm in the lodge, I pray. A lot of tribes have different ways of doing their sweats. Right now my son is hoping to get on at Yellowstone Park. I want him to do what he wants to do. He enjoys the mountains and the outdoors.

"I was very proud of him when he started to dance. He is a Grass dancer, and he is just carrying it on. He explained that he was dancing for his grandmother, his great-grandmother, and me. Having him carry on the ways is important so that it doesn't die out. We made that link so that he will carry it on for our family.

"My grandmother had 14 children, nine of them boys, but she was definitely the one that ruled the family. When she said something, she was the boss. She had 63 grandchildren. She was a very strong woman. A hundred years ago in Montana was what you considered the wild west. Very uncivilized. So she grew up in that time. She died in 1983 when she was 93 years old. She saw a lot in her lifetime, and none of it was ever easy. You survive your childhood, and you try to make a better life for your children. We were a tribe that was able to adapt, there in the mountains, and I am very proud to be Salish."

✳

In 1993, Bobbie's son Michael died when his truck went off a mountain in North Georgia. He had just turned 22. It was very difficult for Bobbie to talk to me about the tragic loss of her son.

7

The Plainsmen

"Michael suffered head injuries in Georgia but actually died in Tennessee. I took him home to Montana to be buried in the same cemetery as my father. At the funeral, when we were singing the 'Home Sweet Home' song of my people, a redtail hawk flew over his grave, and I knew Michael's spirit went with him at that time. Now I carry redtail hawk feathers because that is Michael's spirit. I carry the feather for my son. It had such an effect on my life, I'm not the same person.

"Michael was proud to be a Grass dancer. He had two dance outfits, and we passed them down to other dancers; that way he is still in the dance circle. I carry the redtail hawk fan into the dance circle so he is there with me. Kahoo Burgess, the lead singer with The Plainsmen, our dance group, made a song for Michael when we gave his outfit away. It is called 'Michael's Song.' Kahoo was also given Michael's second outfit. They say that when they sing it, their hearts go in it. Now for me, there is no one to carry on for my family, but I keep helping R. C. Mowatt and The Plainsmen and the younger dancers make regalia so they can carry on for all of us."

Beaded Moccasins

JOSHUA SQUIRREL
EASTERN BAND CHEROKEE

"I DANCE IN REMEMBRANCE OF MY ELDERS

Joshua Squirrel is a member of the Eastern Band Cherokee tribe. The Cherokee, along with the Seminole, Choctaw, Creek, and Chickasaw were highly advanced tribes which became known as the Five Civilized Tribes. Joshua dances the powerful Northern Traditional style, which is not a Cherokee dance, but one which was adopted from the Indians of the northern plains. It is said to have originated with the Omaha tribe.

"I am Bird Clan. I created my regalia. It's hawk and eagle feathers. The colors are symbolic to my tribe. These colors, the black, red, yellow, and white, are in our sacred hoop which is known as the medicine wheel and which represents the four directions. The gunstock that I carry was used in battle. The shield has a turtle for Mother Earth. The shield feather is redtail hawk. The cover is rawhide. The bells around my ankles are for dancing to keep the rhythm. A friend of mine made the moccasins. The fur I wear is ermine.

"I have been dancing about a year and a half. I'm self-taught. I'm from the Cherokee Reservation in North Carolina. I live there and travel around. I pretty much follow the powwow circuit. I travel when I can.

"For myself, for me to do this dance, which is not in my culture, it gives me a feeling. I dance in remembrance of my elders and people who died on the Trail of Tears. It means a lot — the different feelings that I have in my heart at a certain time, and I dance for that. They are always good feelings, not bad feelings. You never take bad feelings in that arena.

"My family is still on the reservation, and they are proud of me. After I took on sobriety, dancing was the challenge. At first it was pretty painful because of the weight of the regalia. To me, if I could conquer the dancing and the pain, then it would be okay.

"At home I dance for special ceremonies. I'm married and have a child, and I will probably teach my little one to dance. The Cherokee don't have this style of dancing, just friendship dancing, and dancing for planting of the seasons, stomp dances. A lot of people back home take on this different style of dancing and they explain what that dance means to them. This is a warrior's dance."

JIM SAWGRASS
MUSKOGEE CREEK

"YOU'VE HEARD, 'GOD WILLING, THE CREEK WON'T RISE.' THAT'S ABOUT OUR PEOPLE."

Jim Sawgrass was at many of the southeastern powwows I attended. He was usually dressed in full regalia amidst an elaborate Creek encampment reminiscent of one that would have been found in the early 1800s. As small groups of people gathered around, he talked about his exhibit.

"It's a small hunters' camp, not a house but a lean-to that the hunters built. A lot of things we got through trade, like cloth, silver, beads, muskets, steel, metal, and traditional tools made out of stone, bone, and shell. This is what this camp is all about. It shows our tribal culture. The lean-to you would build away from the village, and the hunters would use it as they came out. It was mainly for warriors.

"Most of these things I have collected from friends of mine, people in my tribe and my family. And some have been given to me from different people. The fire is a star fire. We use the whole log and put the end of the log into the fire, and as it burns you push the log in, and it keeps you from chopping up a bunch of firewood. Very practical. The Creek hunted deer, and we were fish-ermen, and we were farmers. Corn was the main thing we grew. We also hunted bear and alligator.

"Metal blades began to replace stone blades when the Europeans came. Our tribes became very dependent on metal trade goods. By the 1800s, it was a necessity in the tribes to have hatchets, knives, and guns. In a way, it was the downfall of the Indian people, because they were now dependent on trade goods. The same thing is going on now down in South America today. The tribes are just now getting used to metal items, and very quickly they are becoming dependent on things they can't make for themselves. You can imagine using a stone tool and all of a sudden getting metal.

"We did basketry. We used split river cane and pine needles. Some palm fronds. We made woven mats. When we took something from the earth, we used everything, every single part. With animals, the bones are used for tools and weapons, the meat for food, the skin for cloth-ing and pouches."

Jim is an educator. He is on the Governor's Council in Florida for the Florida Creek Tribe. The Muskogee

"The regalia would be used at stomp dances, the dance that we do. It's a type of stomp; each foot stomps, one after the other. The lead singer, which we call the Yahola, he would use a turtle shell rattle and he would lead the dance with a rattle. But he didn't make all the music; most of the music was made by the women wearing a set of turtle shells on each leg. Usually they wore about seven on each leg, maybe more, filled with seeds and pebbles, and when they'd stomp, they'd make a sound.

"In our stories of the Keeper and Mother Earth, the turtle in our legends is part of creation. The turtle came up and let all the animals crawl on his back, and then he became the earth. The turtle we use for rattles because it represents old age. It is one of the oldest living creatures there is today. This is actually a box turtle, more in the gopher turtle family.

"Our dances are done in a group. Instead of a circle like the Plains Indians, our dances were done in a square, a square-shaped arena representing the four directions of the Earth. And within that square we danced in a circle around the sacred fire.

"There were certain dances that just men did. This outfit would be for a stomp dance or a really important ceremony. You see these pieces that are carved out of shells; way back thousands of years ago, they were what we wore to show rank in the tribes. Later on they started wearing the silver crescent pieces. They actually came from the Spanish and French clothing. When contact was made with Europeans, the clothing changed a lot. Now we had beads, pretty cloth, silver, along with muskets.

"There was also a war dance that we did and ceremonies done before going into war. One was taking of a drink called Osee which is a type of tea we took from the Yaupon holly plant. This special tea would make the warriors regurgitate, which cleansed their bodies before they went into battle in case they were to meet their death.

"My spider earring is from legend. He was the one that brought us fire thousands of years ago — the water spider. The circle with the cross in it represents the earth, the four corners of the earth. And actually that cross represents the square ground in our village. The sacred fire had four logs coming out of it, representing the cross. It's also known now as the medicine wheel.

"We originally had four clans. A clan is what your mother's family is. When you're born, you're born into her clan. When you marry, you have to marry outside

Creek are indigenous to Georgia and Alabama. "When the English came into this area, they called us the Creek Indians because we lived along rivers and creeks. The real name of the tribe was Muskogee. Quite a few broke away and came into Florida, and they were the Miccosukee, a broken-off part of the Creeks. Another group came down and became known as the Seminole, which means 'the people that broke away and lived away from us.' They became isolated and later became their own tribe. During the Creek wars, quite a few were left in Alabama and the Florida panhandle, the ones that didn't get sent to Oklahoma, and that's what makes up the three tribes in Florida today.

"Most of my regalia was made by myself and family and friends. I designed it from old pictures and paintings, and I've made it as authentic as I can. It will never be finished. It's dress-up clothes, ceremonial — not something we would wear hunting.

Woven pineneedle baskets

your clan. If you're male, you marry into the woman's clan. And you take her clan, and your children will take her clan. We originally had four clans in the old days — the deer, the bear, the wind, and the bird. My clan is Bird Clan. I've been told that there are now about 72 clans of the Muskogee people. And a lot of these clans branched off. There are also Muskogees in Oklahoma. They are the ones who moved there in the Trail of Tears. A lot of people automatically associate the Trail of Tears with the Cherokees, but the Trail of Tears referred to every Indian tribe that lived east of the Mississippi River. In the late 1800s, the U.S. was still moving tribes to the west. At one time there were 13 dialects to the Muskogee language; today there are three left that are still spoken.

"My neckpiece is a deer horn with a panther head carved in it. We have a legend about that also. All the animals were put to a test to see which animals could stay awake for four days and four nights, and the ones who could do it the full amount of time would be given a certain power. And each night some of them fell asleep. But after four days the only ones that stayed awake were the panther and the owl. And their gift was to be able to hunt at nighttime when the other animals were sleep. Other animals hunt at night, but they don't have the full power.

"The other part of that legend is that plants were put to the same test and the ones that survived the whole four days and didn't go to sleep are what we call the wintergreen plants. Their gift was to be able to keep their leaves year round. Medicines that come from those plants are what we call the stronger medicines.

"My headpiece is a turban. It is one of the many types of Creek headpieces. We have many types of haircuts. The turban was worn in the early 1800s, and these feathers are egret and ostrich. The ostrich plumes were traded because they were popular with soldiers and for ladies' hats. Each feather has different meanings. The war bird in our tribe was the woodpecker because of its colors, red and black. Western Indians wore a big roach [headpiece]. Our's was a small round roach, something that was worn in battle. The green and black beads on my sash are an old design.

"The number four is important. There are four parts of the earth —- the sky, sea, mountains, and land; there are four directions and four parts of life — infant, youth, adult, and elder. My arm bands are to keep sleeves from ripping on branches. Sleeves are baggy to keep mos-

quitoes off. My leggings are made of deer skin. The moccasins are stitched on top in the center, instead of around the outside, because we lived in swampy areas. We put the seam on top of the foot and coat the bottom with resin to protect it from water and from wearing out.

"I have a stone knife with a deer handle tied on with tendons of the deer. The steel knife represents the time after we began trading for steel, and I have one made from the jaw of an alligator, too. When we kill an animal, we are taking something from the earth. And when we take something from the earth, we try to use every part of it, not waste any of it.

"We have a ceremony once a year called the green corn dance — when the new corn comes out. It's the time of the year when we celebrate our new year. Our new year starts with our harvest of corn, and when that time comes around, we have to renew ourselves in our tribe. There are also certain things we do in these ceremonies to cleanse our bodies. We take medicine made from plants by our medicine men. We also have a scratching ceremony where we get rid of the evil blood that is in us. It's not anything bad. And we have a sweat that we do, although very few do sweats now. Mainly that was done by western tribes.

"During green corn we have a four-day fast, which is also to cleanse our body. We also fast from corn for a long time before the dance; that's to remind us of when our people didn't have corn until the new corn was ready. At the end of the four days, our sacred fires were relit. The old fires were put out during the green corn, and ashes were gathered and buried in the mound in the square in the center of our village. Any dispute you have with anyone has to be settled during the green corn dance, and it goes with the ashes in the mound. And if those disputes come up again, you stand to be banned from the tribe. So that was a way of settling things at the end of the year, and you started the new year over again; a new fire was lit.

"Our houses were log cabins with roofs made out of cypress bark. As we were pushed into the swamps, we built houses made out of palm fronds. The fronds were folded in a certain way like shingles on a house, and they'd last about five years.

"There's lots of sayings about our tribe. You've heard, 'God willing, the Creek won't rise.' That's about our people."

PATRICK PIERRE
PEND D'OREILLE

"THE EAGLE IS POWER. THE EAGLE IS WISDOM.
HE'S EVERYTHING THAT YOU NEED.
THE EAGLE KNOWS HOW TO SOAR ABOVE THE
STORM WHEN IT COMES; HE NEVER FLIES INTO A STORM.
WE NEED TO BE WISE LIKE HE IS."

It is an unseasonably cold, rainy day in July on the high plateau at the base of the Rocky Mountains. I am wrapped in a woolen Indian shawl listening to the drums which, after two days, still have not lost any of their vitality. There are several hundred people gathered round the dance circle at the 97th Annual Arlee Celebration in an arbor just outside Arlee, Montana. I finally gain the courage to approach Patrick Pierre, an imposing figure with wisdom and strength matched only by the mountains which surround his home. Pat is the Committee Chairman of the Arlee Celebration. I am honored that he is willing to take a few minutes to talk with me about himself and his people. He is Pend d'Oreille of the Confederated Salish and Kootenai tribes of the Flathead Nation.

"My position with my tribe is I'm the spiritual leader," he says with great pride. "I am at all the funerals and wakes as the spiritual leader. I've done this kind of work for the past 30 years. I have taught for the past 11 years at the Salish Kootenai College as a Native American Studies teacher, teaching language, songs, and traditional ways of our people — teaching young Indian people how to be more Indian than they are now, teaching our language that is very important and powerful.

"I have a lot of positions in our tribe. I am a war dancer at all of the powwows. I'm out there at every session, every drum. I usually make several powwows during the summer and winter months. I live a traditional life. I teach my children and my grandchildren traditional ways of the people. I'm a grandfather 22 times. I have six children. I have three sons that dance; they are drummers. When you hear the Dancing Bear Drum, they are my boys. The lead drummer there is Allen. He is my youngest son, and he's the one they call the Dancing Bear. His nickname was 'Bear' when he was a boy, and when he started to dance, he called himself the Dancing Bear. Then he started the drum group. The drum is the heartbeat of the Indian country. I sing with my boys now and then."

Pat is dressed in deer skin, and he wears a bone breastplate over his cloth shirt. When he dances, he wears

Breastplate of elk bone

Indians because they took the other way. With a lot of Indians like here at the powwow, you can communicate pretty well. You can walk up to a person and start talking to him and know you are going to have a conversation. You go out on the streets and it's completely different. They are trying to fit into a different world, and they'll never do it. It's kind of sad. I'd like to see my people turn back to their traditional ways, follow their culture and be Indian. The Indian is full of love. He loves everybody. He doesn't have any enemies. So whenever you find people having a conversation, two Indian people, you know that they're friends."

Pat offers a vivid example of the traditional ways: "When we are on the dance floor dancing the traditional dances and you see a feather go down and hit the floor, the man that dropped the feather should have no claim to that feather. He should walk away from it. What we do there, what we are supposed to do is let the elders of the tribe pick up the feather. They take it to their home and take care of it, and the following year, when one year's up, come back to the same powwow and hand that feather to somebody that's worthy to have it. Never give it back to the owner.

"It hurts me to see it done wrong because when an eagle drops a feather, he follows that feather till it hits the ground, and when it hits the ground he will circle three times round where that feather hit, and he'll fly away never to come back to that spot again. He never comes back. And if he's got a mate there, she'll go ahead and raise the young, then she'll follow him. And she knows where he's at. So when the eagle loses a feather, it's gone. And if we want to be like that, in the spiritual way, then we should never pick up our feathers when we drop them. Get the elder and let him take care of it. That's the proper way. Too much now when somebody loses a feather, the elder picks it up and gives it back to him. I don't believe in that.

"So this is the thing I like to give to my people. Live traditionally, believe in the feather, believe in the eagle. The eagle is power. The eagle is wisdom. He's everything that you need. The eagle knows how to soar above the storm when it comes; he never flies into a storm. We need to be wise like he is. That is the message I would like to give to my people. Obey what the spirit tells you. The spirit will talk to you, tell you different things. The spirit will tell you what's coming. You better listen to hear that message.

"Indian people, they are spiritual; they listen to the

the headdress of a war chief. His dance stick is wooden. "This wood I found in the mountains one day. I had a vision of this. There are six feathers on there. Four feathers represent the four directions. The two feathers on this side represent the two seasons I favor most. The flags here and handkerchiefs here, they represent the four directions I use as grand entry — north, east, south, west — I honor the four directions as we go around. I started dancing when I was about four years old, and I quit when I was around 27. I just started dancing again about eight years ago. I like to put my heart into my dance. Some of my grandchildren dance. It's a good feeling.

"Indian people today are losing a lot of their Indian ways. Very few people are living totally traditionally and following their cultural ways, and it hurts me very much when I go out and I can't communicate with my fellow

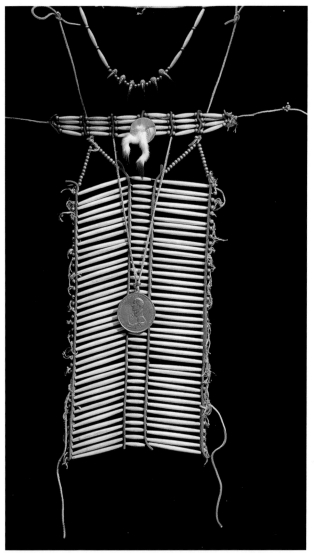

Bearclaw necklace, neck band, breastplate and peace medallion

Pat is fluent in his language. He was taught by his grandmother who raised him. "Indian language is the power of the Indian. If you live it, it's going to come natural. The generation under me, hardly anybody talks Indian. The Indian language is precise, in place, every word you speak, you don't have to repeat yourself."

Pat and the committee he chairs to put together the Arlee Celebration meet once a month during the year. They will begin meeting in July for next year's 98th Annual Arlee Celebration. And plans for a great centennial celebration are already underway. As our conversation slows to an end, Pat takes me aside and points to the mountains and says, "When the clouds clear and the sun shines on the mountain, you can see the shape of a war dancer. That's what makes this place special. Years ago we kind of moved it [the powwow] around a little bit, but for the past 50 years it has been here in Arlee. I've traveled all over the South, East, West, North, but it's always good to come back home."

spirit. The elderly, they live that way. I'm a spiritual person; that's the way I live. I try to share what I have with the people, especially young people. That's the way my dad was to me. He shared everything he knew. When I grew up and had my own family, four boys and two girls, I shared everything I knew with them."

At one time, Pat was a Pentecostal minister. He traveled the Northwest and preached for 18 years. "I preached to the Indian people. I feel that Indian people need to know the other side. The Indian people have always had the great spirit, God; they've all acknowledged it. It was a good feeling to have. It was a good life. When I preached the message, I didn't preach it out of the Bible like the ministry do. I prayed from here [pointing to his heart], then I let the spirit get it out. If we relied totally on books, we wouldn't be Indian."

Rockies, Montana

Chipa and Samson the bear

adaptability for Indian peoples to have social and business relations with the outside world.

"I promote tradition and authenticity in the programs. Tradition is a beautiful thing, but you have to understand that it has always changed. Before Indians were wearing beadwork, they were wearing porcupine quills. There is a great diversity among our Indian peoples.

"My personal love for our native culture is in its communication with and value of the Earth Mother. It is special to me. At one time all peoples had these values; primitive man had to live by the laws of nature. You didn't pollute the waters you drank from; it was common sense. Now business sense takes over, and you pollute the waters.

"The powwows get a good response from traders, craftsmen, artisans, and dancers who create beauty and traditionalism and values. The influences are exchanged. You see a Cherokee out there wearing a Plains bustle. It is that that is creating relations, whether they admit it or not. Powwows are only ours due to the prices that have been paid, the prices like Leonard Peltier and warriors of the olden past, people who fought the Little Big Horn, people who were at Wounded Knee, people who have fought to remain culturally identifiable and traditionally identifiable. I pay tribute to them; I salute the powwows for allowing us to have these things and share them with the world out here. It's because of the sacrifices our people have made throughout time. They would have been washed from the slate had not people stood up for Indian rights and enabled us to preserve these cultural activities.

"Geographics have led to people isolating themselves from one another. When we separate ourselves we become weak. My wife is Lakota Sioux. My philosophy I gain from my Indian identity; cultural ties certainly stem from native philosophies. If we separate ourselves from the earth — the animal, the tree, the deer — then we separate ourselves from creation; and if we separate ourselves from creation, we separate ourselves from the creator. I'm not an overly religious man, but these are the values that I live by. These are the views I have from Native American culture. It belongs to all people, to all animals. Indians have changed with the times, adapted. But we have a relationship as stewards of the earth.

"Last year I did eight powwows. It was way too difficult and expensive. This year I'll only do four. At each

groups in churches and school systems — trying to create authenticity and trying to undermine the fraudulent behavior taking place with all the tribes that are popping up nowadays. There is a real pride that exists, and I want to stimulate that by involving everyone in our circles at the powwows and intertribals. Cross-cultural communication is the best source in bringing about a unity among all peoples. Our powwows and festivals allow for that. I started doing powwows seven years ago.

"We get a lot of response from people on the reservations. Powwows on the reservation for many years remained traditional in their context, and they were not open to public participation. These intertribal powwows, where many tribes come together, create a unity of their own. It's Indians getting along with each other. The participation we get from Indian peoples across the country allows for them to become aware, educated, and involved once again in the outside world. It creates an

powwow we have one host drum and generally have several guest drums. Our powwows are open to as many drums as want to come. The drum represents the heartbeat of the earth. The drum also attracts dancers.

"My powwows are different. Each year I try to implement something new — whether it's Inuit Indians or Aztecs. I think it's inappropriate to create a political soapbox out of powwows. I've tried to create an Indian festival and powwow. I even include other cultures like Polynesian dancers and African Ohuru dancers, and the Aztec Dance Company. It allows for us to include different cultures.

"I don't want my son to grow up with an identity complex. I want him to be proud to be Sioux, Cherokee, and French. We aren't the only ones that have been oppressed, but the government has burdened the Indian people. When we are out there as dancers, as artists, or as performers or speakers, then we are serving as representatives, ambassadors of those people who are left on the reservations, and for the elders. As ambassadors, it's very important that we put our best foot forward to gain respect from the public. We are serving as ambassadors for people who have allowed us to keep the ways alive, the people on the reservations who have kept the songs, these dances. The songs are handed down for hundreds of years. That's what the powwow is. Powwow is preservation, it's education.

"Many powwows call for federal cards. You have to have a card to get into certain events. Mine is not like that. When we do the shows, what we are trying to express is craftsmanship. We do have an arts and crafts regulation; it's a federal law that if you claim the wares are Native American-made and they are not, then it's a violation punishable by jail and fines. If someone is displaying Native American items not made by Native Americans, that information has to be made public. But I don't ask for cards because I know not all the people have them; that's a government thing. We try to create opportunities for our Native American people. We try to have gator tail, fry bread, buffalo, pemmican [a pressed dried meat, usually buffalo, mixed with berries]."

Chipa dances the part of the wolf to Javier Alarcon's hunter. "I am honored to have partaken in that dance with Javier. I am happy to portray the wolf; that's my family's last name. I relate to the animal. With Javier's choreography, it took me about a year to learn. I danced with him about six years. When he was a deer, I didn't see a man dance, I saw a deer. At first I felt inadequate. It wasn't until I became the wolf, which was probably a good year into my dancing, that I understood the dance as a whole. I became a wolf. That was a feeling that went way back.

"George White Wolf made my wolf regalia for me. I was married in it. I watched wolves to get the movements. My Uncle Indio was Yaki, and Yaki was where the deer dance came from. Several other tribes picked up on it. The Yaki are in southern Arizona and northern Mexico. It was a dance favored by them, and others picked up on it. I don't know if Javier picked it up from watching deer. It's incredible. Unfortunately, I don't have time to dance at the powwows now.

"I went to powwows out West and then started producing my own. I felt that I could do it better. I used

Dance leggings

25

to go to some in Gallup and Albuquerque and to the Navajo fair. The Navajo fair was very commercial but yet traditional. They have ferris wheels, cotton candy, yet it's almost all Indian, so it's natural. If you go to Cheyenne and other reservations, you might find more dancing, more bartering, fewer commercial things. In the Northwest Territory with Inuit, Lummi, and Chinook, you run into potlatches, big tribal and inter-tribal dinners, and they are less commercial.

"But you have to be commercial if you have the general public. It costs to bring in dancers, craftsmen, and food. You have to have a paying public. The reverence for the dance does not go out the door, but it has to be more commercial. Our drums, singers, and dancers come to make money. I've been doing the powwow in Canton, Georgia, for five years, and the prize monies are good. They know they will be paid, treated well and fed. It's pretty congenial at powwows.

"Not just anybody can walk up to the drum and sing. Some walk up 'cause they have sung on the drum before. At the 49's guys like to get together and party at night. We want everyone to be able to dance in the circle. The circle is the circle of life. The only problem is that we have people [non-Indian] who come to the powwow and dance in the circle. The next time they have a feather, the next time moccasins, the next time full regalia, the next time they are from a certain tribe, and the next time they have changed tribes. But I don't worry about it.

"We have social dances, round dances, snake dances. Sometimes the dancers compete for prizes. We also can have exhibition dances like the Hoop Dance and game dances like the Wolf Hop. I think it is important to have socials for audience participation. We have to change, to break old habits respectfully, to come together, to overcome the fact that our race has been penalized for their beautiful values.

"Usually I have about 15 competition dances — Traditional, Fancy, Jingle, Grass, and Kids. Three age categories in each one, with the exception of the tots. I try to lend respect to those who have kept the Indian traditions alive. It's not necessarily just the full-bloods who come out there. It's their parents and parents' parents. I see kids out there and think what a beautiful thing to grow up with.

"The circle is sacred. It holds the meaning of everything. Traditionally, you don't have animals in the circle. But I believe that animals are sacred, too. So I bring animals into the circle. I think we are all spiritual leaders. I want us to be popular because of a consciousness of the earth.

"The powwow trail has different circuits. It's become pretty broad. There are a lot of powwows out there. It's becoming pretty saturated. Some powwows even have sponsors like Coors and Coca-Cola, out west particularly. They do powwows for Indians, not necessarily for tourists. It's good. It keeps the social systems intact, the value systems intact. I have a lot of respect for tradition.

"The Cherokee have two different bands, Eastern band and Western band. Clans are like bands within bands. The clan system was more or less to keep genealogy. The clan fell under a maternal system. Cherokee have the long hair clan, the blue clan, the paint clan, the bird clan, the deer clan, the wild potato clan, and the wolf clan. These are all old clans. Many tribes didn't have clans.

"I always try to open powwows, except on school days, with a prayer. The overall idealism of Indian philosophies is the simplicity of spirituality. The Indian people have a direct link, a consciousness with the creator. It's easy to get lost if you have to have a mediator like Christ. Our Indian peoples have a simple, direct relationship with nature and where all these gifts came from — creation, the creator. The relationship with the creator is with us at all times, in all things.

"Something I try to do every day is to cry. That's what I'm made up of. I feel good when I do it. I call it the happy rain. It is my sacrifice. Even on the happiest day, I'll go out back and do that. That's something we have forgotten how to do except for self-pity or indulgence. I have an album that is about to be released that's called 'Tears of Surrender.' That describes what I am doing. It is about giving back. Too many people have taken what is not ours to take. Indian people never had to take because they knew it was given to them. When an Indian went to the woods, the first thing he'd do is pray for the animal that has come and given up his life. It's symbolic. So the deer is not taken, it is given. When we can cry for that consciousness that life has given to you, then that is your only sacrifice. And I enjoy doing it. It keeps me conscious of what's going on out there and it's such a small sacrifice. Consciousness is what we have forgotten as a people.

"I cry mostly for happiness. I love life — that bear, that buffalo, horse, and dog. That's life in its fullest form.

Kristen and Chipa

When it's through with life, it will give itself back to the earth. The earth is the womb of life. And we take a blade to the womb of life and cut it open. 'Tears of Surrender' is dedicated to animals, to trees, to the ones that can't speak for themselves. The ones that can't say 'please don't kill me.' The ones that are lying on the side of the road.

"I have four dogs, a goat, a buffalo named Thunder, a rooster named Five O'Clock, a cat named Fish, a raccoon, and a bear named Samson. He's a Himalayan black bear. He was at a wildlife range. I got him when he was six months old. Part of the range was destroyed, and I bought him. Himalayan black bears are endangered in the wild. There are 10,000 in China in captivity, where their parts are used for aphrodisiacs. Part of my campaign is against that. It's hard for me to buy into a world like that. You know Ghandi said that a government that abuses its animals is no more than pagans."

R. C. MOWATT
COMANCHE

"WE ARE A VERY, VERY PROUD PEOPLE. A PART OF THE TRADITIONS THAT WE FOLLOW ARE RESPECT FOR THE DRUM AND THE WAY WE CARRY THE FEATHERS."

The Comanche were warriors who dominated the Southern Plains. They were a nomadic people, acknowledged as the finest horsemen, traveling their vast land to follow the buffalo, deer, antelope, and elk. R. C. Mowatt is a Comanche from Lawton, Oklahoma. He lives a nomadic life following the powwow trail. He is a powerful dancer, a singer, and the keeper of the drum for his drum [group] known as The Plainsmen. His dance regalia is in the traditional Comanche colors — red, yellow, and blue.

"I designed and made my regalia, and most of my beadwork was made by my companion, Bobbie Orr. To wear a lot of it, I had to gain permission. Years ago, the Comanche only used the otter to cover themselves when they went up into the north country. My breastplate is made of buffalo bone, all black buffalo bone and buffalo hide. The star in the middle was made by one of my aunts before she passed away, and she asked me if I'd wear that star for her. I wear an eagle bustle and carry a dance staff. It has a lot of different meanings to

it. Each of the seven feathers on it has a representation of my uncles — the ones that have passed on, the ones that went to war and didn't come back. And I've got several feathers that were given to me by different people.

"My eagle fan has the meaning of the eagle and the strength behind the eagle. The bird may be dead but its feathers still carry on. There's no misusing the eagle feather because it will always come back on you, back to these feathers. As long as I've been dancing, I've seen what the feathers can do to a person. If you respect them, they will take care of you, bring you out of times when you thought you were really going down.

"I wear ermine tales. A friend gave me two ermines from Alaska and asked me to wear them. I've been wearing them for a long time. I wear yellow arm bands and cuffs. The cuffs have significance of the cavalry. The Indians at one time found it fascinating what the cavalry used to wear. The leggings are Comanche style, made of elk skin and horse hair. The hair represents the horse; the shield represents the armor. When you are out there on the prairie and you face your

of the peyote as a religion. Peyote was used in all kinds of ways. Peyote is like a cactus; it doesn't grow the prickly pears, but it can get big. They naturally call it a narcotic, but it isn't. We used the whole thing; you never waste anything that you take from the earth. That's the way I was raised. The peyote medicine goes all the way to Canada and the West Coast, and it's used in a good way. When we use it in the spiritual way, we always go cleanse ourselves.

"A lot of people don't understand about that religion; when they bring in the staff, when they bring in the fans, the gourds, it's all out of respect for the religion. A lot of Indian people still pray to the Bible, but some don't want it brought into the teepee. There is a significance to the teepee. Teepee openings must be pointed to the east. Chief Quanah Parker was one of the first Comanches to actually function with the white man and let them see a lot about our peyote meetings, our traditions, our ways, our feathers, and so on. They [the white man] tried to Christianize the teepee. Christianizing the teepee can never be done. There were things the older Indians knew even before Christ came, and they talk about that in the meetings. When they brought in this cross and everything, it was just a symbol to follow for the white man. We already had something to follow. Our meetings and the feathers and everything have a lot of meaning to our tribe, and how you carry your feathers and how they are painted and what kind of regalia you are wearing.

"Our eagle feathers, along with a lot of different feathers, are carried down from one family to the next. Some of the eagle feathers that I give away are clean; they come completely off the bird, and nobody has touched them but me. I gave away two particular feathers that went through World War II. They are considered blood feathers because the particular person who was wearing them died for them, and they came back and an elder gave them to me. They are never meant to be kept in a box. That's why I gave them to somebody who can use them.

"In the old days, Comanche women only handled one feather that was given to them by their brother, their uncle or their grandfather. No other person could give them a feather, and they couldn't accept them from anybody else. They use them in a distinctive way and nourish them. My own child has feathers that are a lot older than I am. They were given to me by my grandfather; he spent a

enemy, you want to be dressed the way you are going to die. It's not the pretty colors. The only thing that would pass on out of my regalia is my feathers. All the beadwork would go to the grave with me.

"I dance the Traditional Dance. You pick up your own unique style of doing things. You don't just go out there for glamour. Each movement has a significance of looking for a trail, looking for your enemy, swaying in and out. The uprights represent the quiver of the hunter. I carry a knife — a buffalo-bone, eagle-head knife. I wear beaded moccasins, with elkskin tops and buffalo bottoms."

Once on the reservation, the Comanche adopted the use of peyote in their religion. "We used the medicine lot of years on the road, and he told me a lot about those years. He carried his medicine everywhere he went from Omaha to Montana.

"The particular items that I carry have a lot to do with my grandfather. I didn't speak English until I was in the sixth grade. I spoke Apache and Kiowa Apache. I grew up on the Mescalero Apache Reservation, but then they moved us to a school off the reservation. I was sent to Albuquerque Indian School. My dad was a BIA officer, and that's why we lived on the Apache Reservation.

"There's a lot of significance behind me and the family I'm involved in, because my family and their way of life is extinct to a lot of people who don't see it. My grandmother was on the rooteater side, and my father is from the antelope side. And you have four sectors of different bands that were brought into one area. You have to know what each carries. There's a lot of things our tribe has. They are really strong in their ways.

Medicine wheel

The head chairman of our tribe is Wallace Coffee, my mom's first cousin.

"We are a very, very proud people. A part of the traditions that we follow are respect for the drum and the way we carry the feathers. There's a lot of the unity that goes into the arena. It's a feeling of pride, dancing. A kind of a high. Everybody shows their different style of dancing. Traveling the powwow road for five or six years has been fun, seeing a lot of places, seeing a lot of different people.

"I've traced my ancestors as far back as Ten Bears. Ten Bears was a chief who was known for never turning back and always facing his enemy. The U.S. government killed him. Ten Bears was my great-grandfather."

James "Redblood" Adkins
Chickahominy

"THERE ARE THREE THINGS THAT HOLD OUR PEOPLE TOGETHER—PRAYING, SINGING, AND DANCING."

I met James "Redblood" Adkins at my first pow-wow in Canton, Georgia. I gravitated toward him because of his warm smile and gentle voice. Among the more than 30 booths displaying Indian products ranging from intricately woven dreamcatchers, handmade bows and arrows, and exquisite turquoise and silver jewelry to tasty buffalo burgers and homemade fry bread, he had a small table with stacks upon stacks of recent issues of *The First Americans*, the foremost Indian newspaper. We chatted briefly about the paper, powwow attendance, and the dancers, and he introduced me to his 13 year-old son, Matt, who was dressed in full regalia, ready to dance. Although James was far too busy to be photographed and interviewed at the powwow, we met a few weeks later at the Oglewanagi Gallery and American Indian Center in Atlanta.

James is a Chickahominy, one of the Algonquin Virginia tribes that comprise the Powhatan Confederacy. There is sadness mixed with pride in his voice as he describes his people. "There are seven tribes of us left in Virginia;

at one time there were over 40 but only seven today. We live in the Jamestown area and have a village set up at the Jamestown settlement in Virginia where we show people how it was years ago, how we lived.

"The Chickahominy live on the Chickahominy River. As you come down the James river off the Chesapeake Bay it's a right turn off the river. Three ships landed there in 1607. You know the story of Captain John Smith who was saved by Pocahontas. As the plantations grew, the white man pushed my people back further and further, but we stayed. We are known as 'the people who would not vanish.' We are still there. Leonard Lonewolf Adkins is my uncle, and he is the chief of the tribe."

Indian dance takes place every day in powwows, ceremonies, celebrations, and social gatherings, both public and private. Dancing is a way of carrying on and passing down their traditions, of reaffirming their identities. Most Indians make their own regalia or else wear regalia passed down to them or made by family or friends. James takes pleasure in describing the significance of his regalia. "I usually dress in wool leggings and

Indian dance is rooted in religious beliefs involving the earth, the creator, and the seasons. James travels the powwow circuit keeping his traditions alive and teaching them to his children. "When I get a chance, I dance, and my son dances also. It's a spiritual thing for us. We dance the intertribal and traditional dances because I'm a traditional dancer. Our people also have what we call a blanket dance, a corn dance, a snake dance, a rabbit dance, and of course traditional warrior dances. We danced before going on a hunt, after going on a hunt, after harvest, and sometimes just for fun.

"Each dance has a significance. The dances are passed down to each generation. My knowledge is from my parents, elders, grandparents, and my people. We have our own festival the last week of September. It's the big fall festival— our time for going home. We also have a spring gathering and summer gathering."

Music is an important part of Indian tradition. The drum, the flute, and the whistle are all part of this tradition. James has recently begun playing the flute. "My cousin made my flute for me. He's Pueblo Chickahominy. He gave it to me last September. I had never played one before, but he told me to play from my heart, so I prayed and I began to play the flute. I was very close to my mother. After her death I made a flute album for her called 'Crossing Over to the Other Side.' When you cross over to the other side, whose hands will be out to greet you?

"The flute has been a tradition to my people since the beginning of time. There were always flute players in the village, and groups got together and played. A young man might play the flute to his love, or it might be played to soothe the heart during hard times. Drums and flutes were always there because they were handmade. You would ask the tree for permission, you would make the flute, and you prayed."

Like most Indians, James has seen a great deal of prejudice against his people during his lifetime. "Our people have gone through hell. The war stories I was told by my family and our chief and from other Indian people over the past 40 years make my heart heavy for how my people have not been recognized. It has been said that there are two classes in Virginia, white and colored. Years ago, a white man said there were no Indians in the State of Virginia.

"These are the things I heard, these were the things we had to live through, that kind of prejudice. You are

beaded moccasins. It's an honor to wear beaded moccasins. Wool leggings represent the wool blankets that were given to my people, [blankets] that were infested with small pox. I dance in memory of my people with those leggings. I have a belt made from a rattlesnake I shot about seven years ago on Thanksgiving morning. I ate that rattlesnake and my family ate it so that we could have the spirit of that rattlesnake in us, and so I could wear it on my body.

"The headpiece that I wear is made of porcupine and deer hair; it's called a roach. I have two eagle feathers in the top with a roach pin that holds it onto my head. The shield that I wear is of the turtle, an animal that is of our people. The shield has bear toes and bear claws that represent the turtle bear or bear people. It's a clan in our tribe. My breast plate is of elkbone."

Wood flutes and drum

talking of people who have been in one place for thousands of years. The prejudice is there, you can feel it. It cannot be helped; it just happens. I love my people; I am proud of what I am and who I am, and I will carry on until the day I die. My children will dance and sing and pray, and I hope that my grandchildren will do the same.

"If I could tell the world something, I don't know what I'd say, maybe that I love my people and I am a very proud man. If I could characterize my people, it would be strength, endurance, hardwood, big rocks. Forgive me my tears. Sometimes emotions just come out. There are three things that hold our people together — praying, singing, and dancing. We have always done that."

LEE ANN BRUISED HEAD
CROW

"WE DANCE TO PASS ON OUR CULTURE. CROW PEOPLE ARE VERY PROUD. WE STILL HAVE OUR LANGUAGE. WE STILL HAVE A LOT OF OUR TRADITIONAL CEREMONIES."

When I met Lee Ann Bruised Head she had just finished dancing and was holding her beautiful eight-month-old daughter, Felicia Snow. Lee Ann was raised Crow because her mother is Crow. The tribe's own name, Absarokee, means "people of the bird" or "crow." Her father is Blood, a part of the Blackfoot tribe. Both tribes roamed the plains and prairies of the Northwest. They were hunters of the buffalo, deer, and elk.

The Annual Crow Fair is held the third weekend in August in Crow Agency, Montana. The fair is known as the teepee capital of the world because of its more than 100 teepees. It is a time of feasting, dancing, singing, and parades.

"I am a traditional Crow dancer. I wear an elk tooth dress. I have about 300 elk teeth, and I need to add a couple hundred more lower down. The story behind elk teeth for the Crow is that they symbolize having a rich husband. He goes out and hunts, and you can only get two elk teeth from one elk, so if you have 300 that means he has killed 150 elk. It symbolizes wealth. Today, it is unrealistic to kill that many elk, so they make plastic elk teeth. But some people have authentic elk teeth dresses that have been passed down to them.

"My medallion was made by my great-grandmother. Her name was Florence Realbird. Her Indian name was Baada. That means that she went to a lot of celebrations and she was a real social person. The medallion is special to me because when she made it she was really, really old — she could hardly see. She died when she was 89, and she made it when she was 87.

"The beadwork [on the sash] is Crow design. It was made by an aunt. The way this [piece that hangs down] is slit all the way to the top is significant to the Crow. Crow people are very proud people. You don't go out with just a shawl or with your tennis shoes on; you have to be very properly dressed.

"The Crow people live in southeastern Montana along the Little Big Horn. My grandmother is Lucy Realbird, and she was in this very historical area when Custer was killed. That's where we all lived. We are very traditional and still follow the clan system. I belong to the Big Lodge Clan. We follow our mother's clan.

JOHN PETER PAUL
PEND D'OREILLE

"I'D LIKE MY PEOPLE TO KEEP GOING THE WAY WE ARE. WE ARE PRETTY STRONG. WE WORK TOGETHER."

John Peter Paul is the War Dance Chief at the 97th Annual Arlee Celebration. He is a spiritual leader as well as an elder for his tribe. To interview John Peter Paul is difficult. Several times during the interview, we were interrupted by powwow attendees wanting a photograph of him — and rightly so. He is wearing a chief's headdress, he is an elder, he is obviously, by his position at the powwow, a man of importance. Who wouldn't want to talk with him, to learn from him, to have a photograph taken with him?

"This land is our homeland. The Pend d'Oreille were here before the Salish came. My people have always been hunters. We would go over the mountains to hunt, on horseback. The Blackfoot don't. Later my people became farmers. I used to farm and raise cattle.

"I dance straight war dance. I'm 86 years old. I do a lot of powwows. I traveled as a war dance chief. I was required to go to different powwows. I've been to Washington, New Mexico, and Canada. I was a chief for

dancing. I've been dancing since I was little.

"My dad was dead before I was born. I was raised by my grandfolks. I went to Catholic school through eighth grade, then I went to public school. I didn't go to college. Nowadays you have to have a degree. I encourage all the young people to keep going to school. I've got six children, and they all are college graduates. I have a bunch of grandchildren.

"I am a teacher. I've been teaching for 10 years, mostly language. I'm with the Culture Committee, an advisor. I'm supposed to know everything, I guess. Young people and some older people come to me for advice. I do my best to help people and to promote our culture. I like to tell my people to keep our culture going instead of going haywire. We have been trying with this Culture Committee, trying to teach younger people. I hope they take it and keep it going; otherwise it will die out. I'd like to keep going the way we are. We are pretty strong. We work together."

41

ROGERS CLINCH
WESTERN BAND CHEROKEE

"I AVOID TELLING WAR STORIES BECAUSE . . .
RIGHT NOW WE NEED SOMETHING SPIRITUAL FOR
PEOPLE TO HANG ONTO. I THINK IF I LIVED IN THE
OLD DAYS I WOULD BE A PEACEMAKER."

I met Rogers Clinch in the beautiful Tennessee mountains when the autumn leaves were just beginning to change color. He is a tall, thin man with long, shoulder-length, white hair. I was mesmerized by his soft, melodious voice as he captivated the audience with stories of his people. I asked him how he became a storyteller.

"When I was a kid growing up, people didn't read and write as much as today. There wasn't any television; not too many had radios. So there was a tendency to congregate at certain people's houses, and the older people would talk way into the night, usually in the kitchen around the table. While they were talking, the kids would go out and play. When they finished with the gossip, they would start telling old stories.

"I would rather be listening to the old stories than be out playing, so I sat and listened. I probably got half of the stories I tell from that era in my life. My father had two cousins who were storytellers, and neither married or had children. When they died, I was the one who knew the stories, so people started asking me to tell this story or tell that story. Everyone knew I knew them. It was progressive. I grew into it.

"The youngest story I tell dates back to the time of the removal, so it's roughly 160 years old. Some of them go back thousands of years — we don't know exactly how far back. Primarily I don't tell so much the animal stories that you find in books. I tend to stick to the creation and migration stories or something that ties to them in some way. That conveys a sense of history of the Cherokee people.

"We all have our version of the creation story. There are lots of different versions. Many know their tribal history back to a certain point; like some Lakotas know their story back to a point that says they came out of a hole in the ground. The story does say that, but it was a symbolic thing. The Cherokee story follows that same format, but we have a point in that story where it says we came out of a mound and lay on top of it and dried out. But we have stories beyond that, too, that refer to a place where we held a big ceremony, when we knew that our lives were changing but that didn't really have to do with the creation.

"Also, you take these old stories and go on back with them, and you'll find that there is a creation story very similar to what you find in the Bible, with some variations. Sometimes various spirit forms of today's animals took part in that creation. It depends on the tribe. Sometimes even your own clan will have its own variation. I'm wolf clan.

"The Cherokees have seven clans; some tribes have more, some have less. Some of the stories indicate that maybe there were more clans or families. You are born into a clan. A man in the old days would go to his wife's clan to live. You might have a voice in what went on, but you'd not be in that clan.

"I never started calling myself a storyteller until I was 50. But I've been telling stories for nearly 40 years. I avoid telling war stories because I want to foster the spiritual aspect of our lives, and when you start telling stores about wars, it has a tendency to excite people. Right now we don't need that, we need something spiritual for people to hang onto. I think if I lived in the old days, I would be a peacemaker.

"Storytelling gives me great joy. I travel about nine months out of the year. I do three, sometimes four powwows a month, primarily in the southeastern states. I've been getting calls the last few years to go up north into Illinois, Indiana, Ohio, and I have told stories up there, but since the stories I tell relate mostly to the Cherokee in this area, nearly everyone in the Southeast can relate to them. Nearly everyone claims some Cherokee blood.

"In the old days we had an organized priesthood, and it was the province of the priesthood to tell the stories. But now any Indian could tell a story, and many did. They would often take sacred stories and change the characters or some of the acts in the story so that it was no longer one of the sacred ones, and this is what those stories in the current books are primarily based on. Instead of going to the full-bloods, the researchers would go to the mixed bloods, who were not a part of the really traditional society, and as a consequence they got some stories that were mixed up, some that really don't fit at all.

"This created a sense in the white community that we had forgotten our history or didn't know our history or history wasn't important to us. Just because Cherokees didn't really want to talk about what we call the sacred stories. But they have always been there — hidden in the traditional community. At our stomp dances today, we have men who would be called medicine men who serve the same purpose the priests did. Our organized priesthood was destroyed in 1756; the Cherokee people did that themselves because it had become a very corrupt thing.

"Storytelling is passing down an oral tradition of my people. I am noticing at our stomp ground ceremonies that more and more young people are beginning to listen to the old things. Until just a few years ago the young people weren't as interested as the old people. Now the teenagers are developing a real sense of identity as Native Americans in general, and they are beginning to take pride in their own nation.

"Cherokee is not our name; we have a name for ourselves. A lot of times we use the Creek word that the word *Cherokee* comes out of, but that is the name they gave us. The name we have for ourselves is Aniyunweya. It translates to 'the people of the originator' or 'the people of God.' There are 56 different ways you can translate that, but the most common way is simply 'the original people.'

"Quite a few of the stories that James Mooney collected were written in Cherokee. Incidentally, the translations were not always that good, but they were originally written. Before that it was an oral thing.

"I'm from Oklahoma. Our language there has absorbed names and terminology of the other nations around us as well as from the English. In North Carolina, I found myself very surprised because the dialect is quite different from what we speak in Oklahoma. You can understand one another, but they have sounds we don't have, and we have sounds that they don't have. That is compounded by the fact that in North Carolina they are closer to the original form but they absorbed a lot of the older English terms, what a lot of people consider to be hillbilly, and it sounded strange to my ears. The first time I tried to speak Cherokee there, people told me, 'You sure talk funny.' There is a difference.

"I keep the stories I tell in my head and pick up new ones now and then. For at least 30 years I've done pretty deep research. At first I wanted to cleanse these stories and determine exactly what was Cherokee and what was not. But you can't do that. I found that so many of the stories were so interesting they had crossed the tribal boundaries. You might find the same stories from the East Coast clear to the West Coast, maybe with just a change of character, but essentially the same story. What would appeal to people in one place appealed to them everywhere.

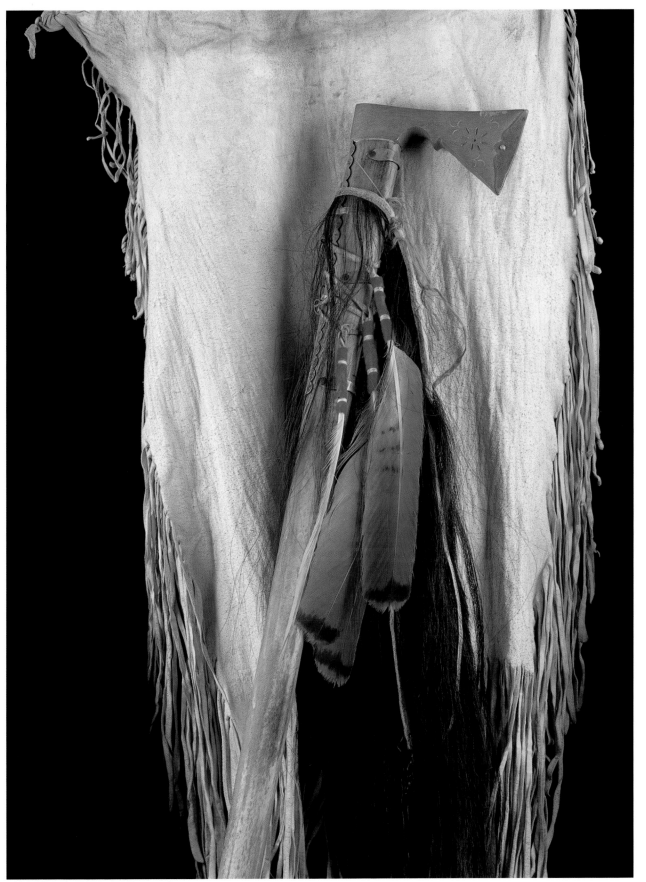

Redtail hawk feathers and dance stick axe

"Sometimes I change the stories when I record them. On my tape, we have a story about the seven brothers, a constellation, but in the recording I changed the name of the constellation so that it wouldn't play into the teachings of a group of people collectively known as new-agers, because they take Indian traditions and try to mold them into their own concept. This has been done in print a lot, and I try to prevent it. As a result, the tape version is not pure, but the way I tell it, that's another matter. In fact, your real traditional storytellers don't tell each other's stories. It's kind of an unwritten copyright law. But still, once you've told one in public and it's been in a book or on a tape, it is considered public domain.

"I use humor, but it's kind of wry humor mostly. It's the kind that comes up and grabs you five minutes after I've stopped talking. Indian stories are always full of humor. There are so many misconceptions out there, and among them is the idea that Indians never laugh, Indians never cry, Indians don't feel pain. The truth is that nowhere is there a more loving people or a more humorous people. Fred Bradley, another Cherokee, and I have on occasion told stories all day long. I truly enjoy a setting like that.

"My favorite story I gave the name 'The Origin of the Strawberry.' It's one that follows the creation story.

THE ORIGIN OF THE STRAWBERRY

Back when there was just one man and one woman on earth, they began to argue, and the woman kept getting angrier and angrier and turned and walked away from her husband. For a time he tried calling her back, but she just totally ignored him and wouldn't look to the left or the right or up or down, just looked straight ahead and kept walking.

They had done this for three days, and the man was following after her and getting very discouraged and his head was hanging down. And the woman in her anger still just kept walking as hard and as fast as she could. On the evening of the third day she was out on the horizon, and each of them camped where they were.

Then on the fourth day, as the sun came up, the woman began her journey and was disappearing from sight when the one that we call Goodmind came down and spoke to first man and asked him, "Does this woman walk in your soul?" In other words, did he love her; we don't have that word. He said, "Oh yes, I wish that I could walk in her soul as she walks in mine." And Goodmind asked him, "Well, if she comes back to you, do you care for her

so much that you'll never argue with her so hard that she'll run away from you like this again?" And first man promised, "Oh yes."

So Goodmind went ahead of the woman and began to plant all of the berry bushes that we know today but that up until then hadn't existed. Still she just ignored them and walked straight on. He began to plant along the path all the trees that bear fruit, like the cherry tree, the persimmon, the plum, and many others. Still she ignored them and wouldn't look to the left or right or up or down, just straight ahead and kept walking.

So, finally, he went ahead of her and planted a big patch of strawberries in all stages of development. And as she walked along, in her anger, she began to step on these ripe strawberries and a good smell came up to her nostrils. She stopped and looked down, and she saw those beautiful red berries, the green leaves, and the white flowers, and she remembered that she hadn't eaten for three days. She was hungry, so she knelt down and she began to taste these berries, and she found that they were both bitter and sweet — like life. She ate a few more.

She looked over her shoulder, and way in the distance she could see her husband coming. She ate a few more and a longing began to grow in her heart to be with him. So she gathered up a handful of the berries and stood up and began to walk in his direction. And every once in a while she would take one of those berries and eat it as she walked along, and each time she did this she would go a little faster until finally she was running as hard and as fast as she could run.

Her husband in the distance saw her coming and ran to meet her. At last they stood face to face, and the woman looked in her hand and she only had one berry left. This she put in her husband's mouth. So it's because of the strawberry that all of us are in the world today.

"And in the old days when we built our mounds, we always faced them with logs, and in between the logs we would plant the strawberries because it was always to be a reminder that people were supposed to love one another. If you look at a strawberry, you notice that the seeds are on the outside, and that's the way our love is supposed to be. So many people, they say they love someone, but they'll never show it. We're supposed to show our love.

"It's also the first of the berry plants to bloom and bear fruit every year. So we have a ceremony as a reminder

Buckskin pouch with bone knife; axe with pipe

that we never let our love sleep. And even today if you go to a traditional Cherokee home, you'll find that the woman keeps a jar of fresh strawberries packed in honey. And if she ever has an argument with her husband, she won't keep it going. She'll go to her kitchen and take down that jar of berries and begin to eat them while she cools down. And when she's calm enough, then she'll get up and she'll take one of those berries to her husband and put it in his mouth and remind him of the promise that first man made to Goodmind in the beginning.

"Not only should Native Americans remember this, but everyone else should too. We so often tell people that we believe that all things are related, that all things are connected, but we don't always practice it. But if we could call that to mind, then we won't make the mistakes that our parents made."

April Renae Wachman
Navajo Western Band Cherokee

"Being Navajo is a tradition of religion. It's up to me to revive it."

The Navajo tribe is the largest in America. The tribe also has the largest reservation, covering most of Arizona and overlapping into New Mexico and Utah. Most Navajo still speak their own language, and many continue to live in hogans, though others are moving into more modern dwellings. With this rich heritage, it is no wonder that April Renae Wachman follows the powwow trail and carries on a traditional life. You can see the wisdom of her ancestors in her eyes, as she speaks of her people, her dance, her future.

"My father is full-blood Navajo, and my mother is half Navajo and half Cherokee. I was born in Utah, and then taken back to Shiprock, New Mexico, where my mom is from, and Farmington — about an hour from the Four Corners. I've traveled around a lot. My mom is a traditional. She does beadwork, and she used to sell artwork. She got me dancing Fancy Shawl when I was about three or four years old. I had been at powwows so I knew what to do. My dad was traditional in all his ways, but I didn't grow up with him. The

powwow world is traditional in its own sense, even though it is intertribal.

"I danced until I was around eight years old, then I didn't dance for about 15 years. About five years ago, I started back dancing because I missed it. I had originally stopped because I cut my hair. There are some people who dance at powwows with short hair, but I'm not one of them. So I waited. When I started back, I had outgrown all my regalia, so I had to start all over. Then, after I had replaced everything, all our stuff was stolen. So I'm making new regalia. I have had to work hard on it because powwow regalia is totally different from my nation's dress.

"In the 1700s and 1800s there was Stomp Dancing, but powwow dancing is more recent. It's a social gathering. At first white people were not allowed to come [to powwows]. Then they opened them up. There are a lot of traditional ceremonies at powwows, like the pick-up ceremony when someone drops an eagle feather. We also have the squaw dance — a ceremony that lasts 14 days — and we also have a sash belt dance that's social. There are eight categories of dance in all.

"There's a story behind the Fancy Shawl Dance. It originated in the '30s and was looked down upon at first, but now it's making a comeback. The story I know well. A woman had lost her husband and had gone into mourning and enclosed herself in a cocoon. Her grandfather came and told her that she was done mourning and that she could go dance again, and that this dance would be for her. So she emerged from the cocoon as the butterfly emerges from its cocoon.

"Our outfits are very colorful. The dance is very quick, like the butterfly. We are light on our toes and move with grace. All my outfits are fully beaded, and you'll see many that are fully sequined cloth. The basic parts are a cape or yoke, or vest; leggings from ankle to knee; moccasins; a shawl; hairpieces; earrings; scarf pins; and slides.

"My next outfit will have cuffs. My mom made the front, and I finished the back. The only thing that is Navajo about my regalia is my concho belt and silver. There is a morning star in the center. It is my favorite symbol because when you wake up in the morning it's the first star you see before the sun rises. So my mom used sunrise colors.

"For Navajos, getting up before the sun does is important. My dad said when you get up with the sunrise it's the best time to pray. Drink water. Think what the creator has given you. When you pray, face east, where the morning star is. So that's what's in the center of my outfit. The shawl is representative of the cocoon as we emerge from it. Some say it is the wings of the butterfly. I wear full minks hanging from my braids.

"Every tribe has its own traditional attire. Before the Spanish came, the Navajo wove their skirts from wool. We would sheer sheep, spin the yarn, and dye the wool. In Navajo the skirts are called beels. They are Navajo rug dresses — woven on big looms that are about six to seven feet tall to make a long dress that's straight and open at the side. They are primarily black with the colors red, white, and green. You close it with a sash belt."

The Navajo are famous for their blankets or rugs, silverwork, jewelry, basketry, and sand painting. Renae is wearing beautiful turquoise and silver squash blossom bracelets. It is said that the turquoise came with the first Navajo people when they emerged from the earth. Although Navajos wore silver, not much emphasis was put on turquoise settings until the turn of the century. "The jewelry I wear is for beauty, it's decorative. It's all turquoise and silver squash blossoms. Turquoise is very powerful medicine. Silver is just an art that Navajos perfected. Navajos make a lot of jewelry modeled on the squash blossom flower; it's a familiar pattern.

"The Navajo were peaceful. We had our enemies — the Apaches and the Utes — and still today we are fighting for our tribal land. But our people were shepherds; we perfected sheepherding. When we are born, we are supposed to be given a sheep, although I was never given one. As we grow older, the more sheep we have, the richer we are. Sheep was food, clothing, you name it. The sheep gave it to us. We didn't idolize them, we utilized them.

"My people speak a dialect that comes from the Athapascan dialect. We helped win World War II because our language is hard to decode. We also have very different foods. Our fry bread is the best, and we have our Navajo tacos. As far as traditional foods go, we have Chilibet, an herbal tea; Chickichin, a red berry that can be picked, harvested, ground, and made into a kind of pudding. These were medicines. We also use blue corn mush in cooking.

"Navajo women are powerful. Everything is maternal in our society. Little girls are pampered. When we hit puberty, we have a four-day ceremony called the kinaalda. Every day the little girl gets up before sunrise and runs, and every day she runs farther. At the same time, a big hole is dug in the ground, about six feet in diameter and two feet deep, and they line it with foil and then

Kachina dolls

corn husks. They make a batter and cook the cake for the four days. Then we are women and we can get married. Traditionally speaking, we take our husband into our house. Navajo women do everything: bear children, cook, clean, harvest. The men were sheepherders.

"The Navajo were put through a removal and hard war. We had a Long Walk from Arizona to Texas. I just don't understand why. Why can't the President ratify the treaties that were first made with the tribe? The Navajo nation is large. Unfortunately, it is growing very quickly, and there is not enough land to put everyone on.

"This year is the first that I have been out of school. I want to be a pediatrician. I want to have my own facilities. I will never turn anyone down. Not many Navajo have insurance. I love children more than anything else.

"I can credit many people for my being here today. Like 98% of today's youth, I was derailed into the white society. I actually believed in a God, the Christian God, and I almost lost myself. I'm glad that I'm living the life I am now, basically on the powwow trail. If there wasn't powwow, I would be struggling. Being Navajo is a tradition of religion. It's up to me to revive it."

CHRISTOPHER PIERRE SAM SANCHEZ
KTUNXA (CANADIAN KOOTENAI) BLACKFEET

"... EVERYONE OF THOSE WHO HAVE EVER
HAD TO ENDURE SOMETHING IN THEIR LIVES
AND HAVE SHED BLOOD, SWEAT, AND TEARS
OVER IT — I DANCE FOR THOSE PEOPLE."

I watched Christopher Sanchez dance for several days before I approached him for an interview. The fact was that he very seldom left the dance arena. He has great strength and stamina, and when he did leave the arena, it was only briefly for rest or water. It is obvious that he puts his heart and soul into every step. His regalia and paint also reflect this same level of dedication.

"I dance what a lot of people refer to as Northern Traditional, but I call it the War Dance. It literally means 'the ones who dance like the old ones.' I had wanted to dance about five years before I actually started because I wanted to earn every one of the feathers. I didn't just get on a list. I worked as a teacher, as a security person for the American Indian Movement, as an educator to native and non-native communities about native issues. And one day my people in my family came and gave me the feathers and told me, 'You've earned these.' So it took me five years from first saying I wanted to dance to actually get started. Everything I wear has significance from somewhere in my family or from someone who has

influenced me or something I want to remember or honor. Since I had to make the regalia, it means something very specific — like from all the times I've gone to work security around drums or pipes or spiritual leaders during events or protests. When you watch the news and on Columbus Day you see a big march and protest in San Francisco, I'm one of the guys out there. I've marched on the border a lot of times.

"This nation, the Kootenai here and the Kootenai in Canada, we got split by the international border. It's a line we never recognized, but it has really torn our community apart. It's caused a lot of animosity, so I always speak out about that. I think it's important for people to know that the Blackfeet Confederacy and the Six Nations and the Kootenai and all, that we never had that line. It's a tool that's breaking us apart, and I think people should know that.

"Traditional dancing is easy since it's a simple step. It's supposed to be an interpretive dance like a Sneak Up or Crow Hop or Straight Song. That's where we pass on our stories and our traditions. It's all real personal. It comes out of your

past, your experience, what you have done. I'm the only traditional dancer in my family, so a lot of the old people ask if I'll dance for them. It really makes it worth it.

"On my dance stick I have an American flag because my mom was in the Army, and I have another one here for the Air Force for my dad. Both my parents were peacetime veterans. My dance stick is an eagle claw. These are buffalo hooves. This talon was the first thing given to me by my family when I first told them I wanted to dance. I went out and fasted once, and this agate came to me, so I put it in there. And all these feathers are from different events, different times that I have worked, different people who have helped me, so I try to keep as many on me as I can as long as they are not getting loose.

"I am now wearing five feathers. Each one is for a time that I volunteered to work security: one time was in Seattle — President Clinton was there, and they let us go within 10 yards of him — we worked security around the drum; one was for Columbus Day in San Francisco; one for marching at Wounded Knee on the 25th anniversary of the takeover; one for marching on the border close to Vancouver, British Columbia; and the last one is for a tribunal at San Francisco. Also, I have my tassel from graduation.

"The red under my eyes is for the blood and sweat and tears the Indian people have suffered through for the last 500 years. From the first Tehanos whose lives were changed by Columbus and the first ships; to the development of international border issues; to American Indian political prisoners; to everyone of those who have ever had to endure something in their lives and have shed blood, sweat, and tears over it — I dance for those people. I don't dance for myself.

"I go and dance in prisons all the time because those people can't come out here and dance. So I say, 'Don't worry, I will go dance a good song for you, and maybe next year we will dance together.' I look at it as a big responsibility. When my uncle came to me and gave me a whole mess of feathers, it shocked me for awhile because it is a big responsibility. And it took me a year before I was really ready. I had to do a lot of praying. I had to go talk to a lot of people. I had to go through a lot of ceremonies to learn how to take care of them. Everyone of these feathers stands for a spirit.

"I have a bachelor's degree in political economy. My original intent was to get into politics, looking at natural resource management and economic development. Sustainable development, development in ways that will not permanently alter our surroundings or deplete them — responsible forestry, fishing, and things like that. Also, I have started a master's program in Vancouver, British Columbia, in political science, looking specifically at resource management.

"Right now I work for an independent school society, and also I am a teacher at East Kootenai Community College. I teach Native studies. Also, I have taught at Northwest Indian College on the Lyn reservation as a political science and communications instructor. My people helped me go through school, so now I'm giving back. That's what I fight for today when I have all this on.

"I go and talk to a lot of young kids and tell them to stay in school. If you don't want to live on welfare and you don't want people to do everything for you, stay in school, get your training. There are all kinds of people to help you do that. Today, we get our money from the government. Tomorrow, our hope is that we'll get our money by ourselves. We'll have sustainable economic communities that aren't based on just gaming, that aren't based solely on welfare, and that aren't based solely on hand-me-downs. To be self-reliant, responsible, educated people — that's what we want.

"When I hear people talk about other tribes as our traditional enemies, I don't really believe all that. When you look out here in this arbor, you see Kootenai, Blackfeet, Salish, Cree, and we are dancing together in one circle. And we step on that floor as one people. I always try to tell people, in the old days we may have had

Carved bear fetish

conflicts with each other, but anything that is against sobriety, spirituality, solidarity, and sovereignty, that is our enemy today. Those are the four things that I dance for and respect people for. I don't believe in blaming each other as traditional enemies because we all have to work together to step into the next generation.

"I talk to a lot of students and young people about the concept of identity. My father is Ktunxa, the Canadian Kootenai from British Columbia and Alberta, and my mom has decendency from Blackfeet. My dad was taken out of his family and didn't know where he was from, and my mom's family doesn't really know where their Indian blood comes from. I talk to a lot of people about how I felt at not having that identity and what I had to go through tracking down who my parents' parents were. And I always talk to them in a real respectful way because a lot of things are real hard for them to talk about. When they went to school, they had their tongues branded with irons if they spoke in their own language, they were beaten and ridiculed for practicing their own ways.

"A language is everything. People use their language to talk about where they are from. They use it for place names. That in a way creates a sense of identity. We came from the area of the two lakes; that's how we remember it. And when someone comes in and completely changes that, it's like coming and telling us that we don't have a history, like we don't have an identity."

ANTOINE CANTSEE
UTE

"THE BISON HEAD ON MY SHIELD IS VERY SPECIAL."

When I met eight-year-old Antoine Cantsee, he was very excited — he had just won the Special. He is a Junior Boys (ages seven to eleven) Traditional Dancer. He is wearing full regalia in yellows, blues, and black, and he wears a large porcupine hair roach on his head.

"I've been dancing since I was three years old," Antoine says. "My mom made part of my outfit; she did my beadwork. The bison head on my shield is very special. We traded for my bustle, and it will be handed down. I'm holding braided sweetgrass in one hand, and I have a dance fan in the other. My tribe is Ute."

The Ute are considered a Great Basin tribe. The state of Utah is named for them. Due to their proximity to the Plains, they adopted many of the traits of the Plains Indians. The Utes were hunters following the deer and antelope herds.

DAMION TOINEETA
EASTERN BAND CHEROKEE

"I ALWAYS FEEL GOOD AFTER I DANCE."

Damion Toineeta is a burst of blue and white as he swiftly goes through the intricate footwork and exaggerated body and head movements of the Fancy Dance. Fancy dancers elevate their feet and legs in a much more dramatic style than Northern Traditional dancers. The Fancy Dance requires stamina and balance, and some Fancy dancers incorporate acrobatic flips and splits into their routine.

Damion wears the signature double bustle of hackle feathers on his back, as well as arm bustles. He carries wands with white twirlers, and on his head he wears a roach with rockers. Both are designed for movement, to show that he is keeping time. His blue and white regalia has long white fringe that catches the eye as he stops, starts, and spins to the fast-paced beats of the drum.

"I've been dancing for about six years. My mom made my regalia. I feel different every time I dance, but I always feel good after I dance. My brother dances, too; he's a grass dancer. He taught me the basic steps, and then I watched other dancers to learn other steps. Now I dance just about every weekend."

CLARK MATT
SALISH

"MOST PEOPLE GO TO POWWOWS TO HONOR TRADITION. POWWOW IS A PRAYER. YOU DANCE FOR YOUR PEOPLE."

When Clark Matt enters the dance arena, all eyes are on him — he is wearing a bison headdress. However, as we talk, he admits that he doesn't always wear it because it sometimes scares little children. "The bison headdress was made by my nephew, and he gave it to me a few years back. A lot of times I wear a high top hat. The oldtimers wear a hat all the time. They wear it to traditional events. Those high tops are hard to come by anymore, and they cost a lot of money.

"The horn I carry is elk horn, from a big prize elk. That horn was a natural drop off of the elk antler. The animal spirits were given to our people a long time ago. That was before we got into Christianity. We prayed to the animal spirits in everything we did. The bird is sacred. The elk is sacred. The buffalo spirit is sacred to us. When we got into Christianity, we kind of lost the old ways of following the spirits. In the winter months we have our ceremonies, and each tribe does its own dance, but most of our people are Catholics.

"My breast plate is made out of bone; I made that myself. This here is a medallion. My gloves are old, handed down. They are old cut beads. They belonged to my dad's dad, and they've been handed down in my family a long time. I don't wear them that much. The bridge cloth is made by my mother, the beadwork and all. My sister made the leggings. Then I worked on my bustle. The fan was given to me by one of my brothers, too. In my hair I wear otter. It came from a very special old Flathead woman; she can't dance anymore so she gave it to me. It's otter skin for wrapping your hair. This is a pipe bag. To be a pipe carrier, you have to earn it, to follow certain steps. Each tribe does it different.

"We dance counterclockwise, the opposite way from the usual, to protect what we do. Most tribes dance clockwise, but we dance our own way to protect what we have. We keep the tradition to our people.

"We originally came from the Bitterroot Valley down by Stevensville. Then the government moved us toward Missoula and then where we are now. Each time they moved us north. They moved the Kalispell and Pend d'Oreille. The Flathead Lake used to be called Pend

"The Salish practice a lot of crafts. A lot of our people do beadwork, bows and arrows, and bark baskets. Some make a living tanning hides. Most people go to powwows to honor tradition. Powwow is a prayer. You dance for your people. We have a memorial, and we think about those who have gone on. Pray for them. Or you pray that everyone has a good time. A lot of people just dance for fun. At some powwows, you have to have a number to dance; it's a contest. The Council runs the tribe — the older men. They are supposed to guide the reservation. A long time ago, we had different chiefs for different things, like the chief for war dance, chief for firewood, chief for hunting, chief for women to gather berries. Our people used to follow the herds. We followed the buffalo back and forth. We still hunt elk, moose, and deer, but we cannot hunt the buffalo except certain times of the year. The Bison Range gave us buffalo meat for this powwow.

"When I grew up, the elders wanted you to learn the old ways, and now it is the Tribal Council that wants the people to learn, especially the language. I teach my boy the songs. We have different ways and traditions. You have to do certain things in a sweat lodge, you have certain ways of the pipe, certain things to do in the winter months, which are sacred to us, when the snow comes. How to take care of loved ones when they die, until you bury them. You teach children the circle of life, that everything we do is a prayer. That's what we teach our children. My son dances off and on; he started dancing when he was small. My daughter has also danced traditional.

"You need to come to the reservation to know our people, our Indian way of life. Because if you are not around Indians, you don't understand what the Indian is all about. We are known for our gentle qualities. Everybody will invite you over and feed you on the reservation. The mountains are sacred to us. You can see the dancer on the hill. The people are like the land. We are part of the land, and we don't take it for granted. We pray for Mother Earth all the time.

"I go back to the Bitterroot Valley some, but the land has changed a lot. When I grew up, we saw buffalos and Brahma bulls. The Indians and whites could ride the train for free. We've heard the stories about a long time ago when cattle men and sheep herders got into the fight. You don't forget stories because the elders tell you over and over. Hearing and remembering the old stories is another part of our lives."

d'Oreille Lake. The Flathead people are friendly. We have Crow, too.

"We all travel around to different powwows. I've danced in different places around Browning, in Washington State and Canada. I've been dancing 13 years. I started when I was small, and then I quit, and now I've started back up again. When I first started dancing, I danced with a hawk bustle. I was probably one of the first to do that, to dance with a hawk bustle, before the eagle bustle.

PAUL DE LUNA
APACHE TUSCARORA

"POWWOWS HAVE BEEN A TEACHER TO ME, A GREAT TEACHER."

Paul De Luna is a craftsman, and I was attracted by his display of fine flutes and pipes. He travels the east coast as far north as Michigan and Minnesota, and in the winter returns to Florida.

"My mother was Tuscarora; my father was Apache. I grew up in Texas, but I lived all over. I travel year round; it's a full-time job. I've been doing it for five years now, traveling and making a little bit of everything. I am a jewelry maker, I do some painting and carving, I make dreamcatchers, bows and arrows, also the tribal stick. I paint the shields.

"Most of my stuff is taken from many different tribes. For example, there are several legends attributed to different tribes for dreamcatchers. And red cedar — I like to use it because Indians in the early days used it a lot. They believed it had special properties because of its aroma. So I like to use it to make pipe stems and flutes, also rattles. Most traditional stuff was not quite as decorated as my stuff; it was just a little leather and feathers.

"The Apache, Zuni, Navajo, a lot of tribes of the southwest used flutes quite a bit. It's been traced back since the beginning of time. Anasazi, culture which was the pre-

decessor to Navajo and Zuni, had cave drawings of Kokopelli, who was the music spirit, the character playing the flute. So it dates back as far as anyone can tell.

"I grew up in the suburbs and didn't know a lot about my Indian heritage until I was grown. I've been discovering it ever since. Powwows have been a teacher to me, a great teacher. For the people who work it, as well as the general public who view, it is a way to learn something new all the time, because you meet different people from other tribes and learn history from those who know more.

"This was not my life plan. I went to a powwow and really enjoyed and struck up a friendship with the person who put them on, and he invited me out to more. He asked me if I cared to participate as a vendor and gave me ideas on things to put together. I tried it, I enjoyed it, and I've been hooked ever since. My personal favorite is carving knife handles because it allows me to do intricate work. I use deer antler and bone. I carve all kinds of patterns — eagles and wolves — into them.

"My parents are proud that I'm doing this. They love to come to powwows, too. I have a younger sister and

two older brothers, but I'm the only one involved in this. I go to the dance ring occasionally, mainly for special occasions. I don't have regalia yet.

"I picked up carving myself. I find pieces of wood or bone or whatever and study them for awhile and see what comes to me — what I can see myself making out of it. Before I actually started doing this as a living, I did it as a hobby. I love to do carving and artwork. I do it because I enjoy it.

"In doing decorative pieces you have to be careful. Tradition varies from tribe to tribe, and I try not to do anything that would offend any particular tribe. For example, feathers are important, and I try to use them in some pieces, but their meaning can be very different. Another example is red catlinite, a type of stone which some people use. It's very popular to make pipes out of. But the only problem is, some tribes consider it a sacred stone and feel that it shouldn't be used. So mostly I use deer antler and sometimes soapstone, a soft stone.

"I also enjoy music very much. I'm not a very good musician, but I appreciate others who are. I play the flute a little bit. That's one of my ongoing projects.

"I think that everyone should take great pride in their own culture, but I think we should take the time to explore all cultures because I think it helps us respect the way other people are more. The more you understand, the more you respect. To prejudge any culture before learning about it is a terrible thing. There's too much of that going on. On television, the movies, we get these set ideas about the way things are. I don't think anybody should take these ideas to heart. Indian people vary just like any other people.

"I do my work because I enjoy it, but I hope it brings other people happiness. When they come and buy a piece from me, it makes me glad that they appreciate it enough to purchase it and will enjoy it for a long time. Hopefully, even long after I am gone, they'll still have it. It is my legacy, so to speak, that will live on."

Hand drum

DIAMOND BROWN
EASTERN BAND CHEROKEE

"THERE'S A CONTENTMENT, A PEACE IN MY HEART WHEN I RELATE TO THE OLD WAYS."

Diamond Brown is a dancer, a teacher, a story-teller, a spokesman for his people. He travels the East Coast giving presentations to schools, to Scout groups, to private groups, to anyone who will listen. He is carrying on his traditions in the best possible way — teaching. I saw him mesmerize a group of first-grade Tiger Cub Scouts for over an hour with the stories of his Cherokee people. They didn't move; they listened and they learned. And as a dancer he is without peer. His movements are precise and strong.

"I enjoy dancing. I am a Traditional dancer. I am a warrior for my people, in regalia and out of regalia. I fight for Indian issues. I believe in what is right for the Indian people. I was brought up on the reservation and raised an Indian and to be proud of what I am — and I am proud. I came off the reservation to look for work, to do better for my family, for my people.

"I'm not so sure that I am doing better. I've learned a lot being off the reservation, but I've missed out on a lot. I can do a lot for my people on and off the reservation, but I feel a stronger need to be there for my people. There are

more of us there. My parents live on the reservation, my whole family does. Things are different than they were 200 years ago, even eight years ago. Right now is the time that Indian people have started to grow in harmony even more than they ever have. The Indian people, the Indian culture is very strong. Being a warrior, I need to get back.

"Before I put my paint on, before I even knew how to paint, I had to pray to the Creator, and the Creator told me how he wanted me to paint. That's my identity between me and him. So if I go into battle, naturally I'd be wearing my paint, and if I were to die, then he [the Creator] would see that it was me by my paint. I can't change it. It was given to me by him. He will recognize me and take me into the spirit world.

"I paint my face black, white, and red. Those are my colors. The black represents death. I'm a warrior, and I'm going to go out and fight for my people. If it means giving up my life and dying for my people, then I will die for my people. The white represents peace and serenity. When I go out, I'm hoping for peace and serenity. I don't know what the outcome will be. The red means

Brooke Brown

goes, she takes first place in her category. The Jingle Dance represents a prayer. It is not a Cherokee dance; in fact, most of today's dancing is not Cherokee. We still do our Stomp Dances and Green Corn Dance, but this dance comes from a tribe up north. The story behind the Jingle Dance is that once a little girl was very, very sick. Every day her grandfather would pray for her, and every day that he prayed, he would twist up a cone. After 365 days of praying for her to get well, they put all those cones that he had twisted up and made her a dress, and they got out the drum and started singing prayer songs. The little girl got up and put the dress on with all the jingles on it, and she started dancing, and after the song was over, the little girl was well.

"I have another little daughter, Wahlalah — that's Cherokee for 'hummingbird.' She is only four, and she has been dancing since she started walking. Right now she is doing a Traditional Ladies Dance, but she prefers the Fancy Shawl Dance because it is a faster, upbeat type. If we are doing a program or exhibition, she dances Traditional, but if she is at a powwow for competition, she does Fancy Shawl. Wahlalah is a good dancer. She's in Tiny Tots where all the little children are winners, but eventually she'll be a champion dancer also.

"My wife makes all their regalia. She has just finished up another regalia for Brooke, and she's been working on it for a year and a half with a lot of beadwork. It takes a long time for these things.

"At the present time, Sandy doesn't dance, but she's going to be a Traditional dancer. She hasn't gone out and danced on the trail yet, but at the powwow coming up on Mother's Day, they want her to be head lady dancer and me to be the head male dancer. Sandy wants to dance in her heart, but she's afraid what other people will say. She's part Indian, but a lot of people have come out of the closet, and all of a sudden they are Indian.

"These people coming out of the closet, they hurt the other Indian people. They want to get in on benefits. The real Indian people, they're going to be the ones left out once again. The ones not in it for the benefits are in it to feel important. I've talked to a lot of skins about why these people want to be an Indian, and we feel that, among their own race, they feel they have missed out. They are searching and want to be important somewhere, some way, somehow. So when they find out that their great-great-grandmother was Indian, they jump up on that horse and pretend to be an Indian. I talked to one guy who had tried

Indian people. Their dance is a prayer. Movements have a special meaning to me.

"My three daughters dance. My wife, Sandy, and I taught them how. Brooke is 12 years old. She began dancing several years ago, starting out with the Fancy Shawl Dance, which represents the butterfly. She took first place at the Cherokee dance on the reservation in her category at the 4th of July powwow. At Raccoon Mountain this past fall, she was crowned a Rolling Thunder Princess. She is really a unique child, not just because she is mine, but she is a good girl, with good qualities about her.

"She's real special. Sandy and I feel that she is our miracle baby because when she was born she only weighed a pound and 11 ounces, and she was born on the reservation. Being that small, they had to take her to another hospital with better facilities. While we were waiting, I had to hand pump a machine to give oxygen to her. I had to do this for hours just to keep her with oxygen.

"I have another daughter, Dakota, who'll soon be seven. She's a Jingle dancer and also a champion; everywhere she

Dakota Brown

the motorcycle thing and that didn't work, and now he wants to be an Indian.

"I dance from my heart. I let my heart do the speaking. I don't think with my mind; I think with my heart. You have to understand that my people, not just the Cherokee but my race of people, had no hunger here, no homelessness here; we had no jails, no prisons, no policemen, we had none of that. We thought with our hearts instead of our minds.

"At the same time, that drum will move you. There are many, many, many times that I will be dancing and that drum moves me. I will try to push my feet down upon Mother Earth, to touch Mother Earth, keeping in time with that drum, that heartbeat, and it just seems that Mother Earth is pushing my feet back up. And I push them down, and Mother Earth pushes them back up. It's like walking on clouds. Dancing is a way that I pray. It's another form of prayer for me. That's my way, the old ways. There's a contentment, a peace in my heart when I relate to the old ways. I want to keep our culture alive and hang on to my traditions. I want my children to also; I want it to live."

SHAUN ADAMS
CREE STONEY

"WE ARE STRONG BELIEVERS IN OUR CULTURE."

Shaun Adams is a Grass dancer. Grass dancing is somewhat similar in movement to Fancy dancing; in fact, some people even say that Fancy dancing stems from early Grass Dances. Like Fancy dancing, Grass dancing is strenuous; the fancy footwork and body movements require great stamina. Shaun wears dramatic blue and white regalia with long fringe. There is a thunderbird on his breechcloth.

"My mom made me this outfit so I could dance. Where I come from, the eagle represents the thunderbird. The thunderbird is one of the most highly respected grandfathers an Indian could have. The blue represents the sky; the white, clouds. My dance staff is a medicine ring. The sweetgrass is to protect me.

"This is only my fourth time dancing. My brother taught me a few moves, but the others I learned from other dancers, and I've practiced. My grandfather used to dance, but he passed on two years ago. I go to powwows in Alberta and British Columbia. I'm from the Paul Band Indian Reserve 45 minutes west of Edmonton. There are many Cree reservations."

Shaun is Cree Stoney. His father is Stoney, and his mother is Cree, one of the major tribes in Canada. "The Cree were warriors, but we didn't make trouble. We are generous people. We are hunters. We go for everything from the bull moose down to the chicken — whatever we could find. The Cree came from the States but went up into Canada. We are strong believers in our culture. We mainly go to Sun Dances, and we talk a lot about our heritage. The Cree language is still spoken. I'm trying to learn it."

PETER SOBACK REDBIRD
OKLAHOMA SEMINOLE CREEK

"AS LONG AS OUR CEREMONIAL FIRES ARE RENEWED EACH YEAR, OUR PEOPLE WILL LIVE FOREVER."

I heard about Peter Soback Redbird long before I met him. One day I went into the Silver Sun Gallery in Atlanta, which his mother owns, and heard her talk of her son who was dancing at the Red Earth Festival. She offered me a warm buske, a traditional drink of her people, made from parched corn. Later, when I caught up with Peter for an interview, he talked of his traditions, his family, his dancing, and his art.

"I am Oklahoma Seminole Creek, the Mikasuki Band. Most tribes have bands or clans. When we first came to the Southeast after the Creator first blew away the great fog, each group of people that clung together swore eternal brotherhood, and we took on Etowah names, and we were given specific jobs in our community. For example, my clan is the Bird clan, who were messengers. They would relay information between different groups. The Alligator clan took care of the dead and made sure that all preparations were made for burial. The Panther clan were our military leaders; they planned our moves and stuff like that. The Wild Potato clan took care of our horticulture, the farming and stuff.

"We were never allowed to marry someone in our same clan. We saw that as inbreeding. The husband moves in with the wife's family. The Creek and Seminole, we are actually Muskogee. That's what we call ourselves. It means 'lower valley people.'

"The Trail of Tears removed all Native Americans in the Southeast to Oklahoma Territory. Our capital is in Wewoka, which is where I am from. There was a small band of about 200 people who stayed in Florida and hid out. They were Seminole, Timuqan, Mikasuki, and other small groups of people. In 1973, the state of Florida granted them state recognition because they were about to be eliminated, and then they got federal recognition, so today we have a Florida Seminole tribe and an Oklahoma Seminole tribe. But we are two separate nations, very different.

"Most of the time when you say Seminole, people automatically think Florida, but Florida has only 3,000 tribal members. In Oklahoma we have over 14,000 tribal members and over 30,000 Creek members. There are about nine active Seminole clans today, and all are members of

VIRGINIA VILLAREAL
WICHITA AZTEC

"MY MOST IMPORTANT NEED RIGHT NOW IS FOR US TO START TO BE AWARE OF MOTHER EARTH."

It was late in the day, a few hours before sunset. I had been at the powwow all day and finally decided to relax and browse among the more than 30 craft booths. I almost walked right by the small space occupied by her gallery, but something caught my eye — a stick with beautiful beadwork and macaw feathers. As I walked in I was greeted with a broad, welcoming smile and the words, "Touch anything you want to; this is a touching gallery." It was Virginia Villareal speaking, and she truly meant what she said. Her beautiful objects are meant to be touched, to be held, to be cherished.

"They need to be touched; that's what they are for. They are not there to hang and to be lost. The talking stick is one familiar to my father's side. My father, Joseph, was Wichita, and my mother, Aurora, is Aztec. The talking stick was used primarily in counseling with the younger. They were allowed to speak only with that stick in their hand. A talking stick was nothing more than a plain piece of stick that had been found, removed from the earth, utilized to be talked with, and then put back where it was found. Mother Earth was thanked upon its return.

"There you see a fetish particular to the Aztecs. It is an eagle-taloned fetish that has the head of a thunderbird on it, and it is carved in bone. They are for meditation, prayer, for personal use. And sacrificial knives are another part of the fetish.

"When my great-grandmother brought my grandmother up from Mexico, they lived in an enslaved atmosphere. They were brought up by the Spanish that moved up into the area, in San Antonio, where Mother was born. My father was adopted out of his tribe in Oklahoma and brought down into Texas. So they met in San Antonio.

"Both of them worked for Kelly Air Force Base; my father was in construction, and my mother was working in ammunitions. They were having lunch across from each other when he saw her and invited himself home. He was not accepted. He slept on my mother's door sill for three weeks before she consented to have a date with him. By that time, mother had been sold into her first two marriages, and they did not work out. Father was the only one that lasted. They were married for 54 years before my father died eight years ago.

ERNEST NESMITH
COMANCHE

"EVERYONE KNOWS THE COMANCHE . . . THE BEST HORSEMEN ON THE PLAINS."

Ernest Nesmith was the first Native American dancer that I met. I watched his exacting dance movements in the arena as he recreated a warrior preparing spiritually for a battle. Afterwards, I approached him and was rewarded by his friendliness and openness. He is a Comanche, born in Texas, but with family in Oklahoma.

"Some of the pieces I wear are personal. When you make your outfit, a lot of thinking and time go into it. I've been told how to make certain things, what colors to put in it. Everyone has a different outfit to fit the dance. You have to remember that I am a Northern Traditional dancer, and we are a Southern Plains Tribe, and that is incorporated into my own personal style.

"Each tribe has its own songs, its own ceremonies. For example, we have a Gourd Dance — an old southern dance from way, way back. The Gourd Dance was the warrior's dance. Nowadays a lot of elderly people do it, and young people do it. Back home our powwows are mainly family dances that start off with the Gourd Dance. We do that for a couple of hours, then we start other dances.

"This [headpiece] is a roach. It is made out of porcupine quill with dyed deer tail. It's actually the guard hair of the porcupine, and underneath it we have dyed deer tail. Inside are two roach feathers. This medallion is a gift given to me by my cousin. My breast plate is for protection. It is out of buffalo bone or deer bone with leather in between.

"These are the colors I have chosen to dance with. They are Comanche colors — red, yellow, and blue, which represent blood, sun, and water. I have taken those colors and added them to my own beadwork.

"My deer hide fringe represents the grass of the plains. The epaulets are of hawk and eagle feathers. My bustle is made of osprey hawk feathers. Traditional dancers use feathers from birds of prey like the hawk and eagle. The eagle is such an honored bird; it is believed that he carries our prayers up to the Creator. There is none stronger than him. There is a lot of medicine behind those feathers. You can use them in a lot of different ways — ceremonies and such.

"The uprights, they represent the quiver and the arrows that would be sticking out of the quiver. I have a golden eagle fan. It has three feathers and a tail. It was

given to me when I was way up in Montana, way up north. I had just started dancing and was using someone else's fan, and a man honored me with it. My dance stick is an eagle claw given to me by someone I consider my brother.

"A lot of things have been given to me, but otherwise I try to make everything. I make it to last, to be up to my standards. I wear paint sometimes. For that you have to be given permission from your father, grandfather, or uncle. I dance for my family, myself, and my friends, but the number one reason is, I dance for the Creator.

"The Comanche were nomadic people; we had a lot of territory. We were mostly Plains Indians: we followed the buffalo, we had summer and winter places, we were a pretty fair tribe. Our traditional dancing included Sneak-Ups, Southern Horse Stealing, Northern Crow Hops, and the Prairie Chicken. When you are on the powwow circuit you realize that a lot of the songs and dances are Plains. We started wearing bells around our ankles to represent that we were dancing in time with the drum. On the contest side of dancing, they notice that.

"I speak a few words of Comanche. A lot of the older people know Comanche, but it is a difficult language. You use your tongue and your mouth in different ways. Everyone knows the Comanche. A lot of people think they were mean and cruel. We were actually the best horsemen on the Plains. A lot of photographers and writers talk about the Sioux. They thought they were the best horsemen.

"The greatest thing was to go on a raid to bring back things, to show how strong we were. They talk about older men, how once they reach age 45 they were too old to go on the long raids and do all the things on horseback.

"Comanche women do Scalp Dances. They are an honor for men and their families. The women had their spears, and they had the scalps representing how strong their family was. Of course, there are different ways the women were honored. There are a lot of Comanche women who dance the Southern Cloth, the Buckskin, the Jingle Dress, the Fancy Dance.

"There are a lot of people I would like to thank for getting me where I am now. We are trying to get our own drum together. Some songs are real old. Some are new."

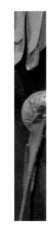

DAN WOLF
LUMBEE WESTERN BAND CHEROKEE

"I WISH I COULD GET IT ACROSS TO THE INDIAN PEOPLE THAT THE OUTSIDE WORLD IS WHATEVER YOU WANT TO MAKE IT."

You can't miss Dan Wolf at a powwow—he's the one with the Brahma bull named E.T. and the colt named Cloud Dancer. Together, they put on quite a show, and they are a crowd-pleaser with the children.

"I was born and raised in Ardmore, Oklahoma. I was there for 10 years, then moved back to my father's homeland, which is in a very small town called Pembroke, North Carolina. And there I stayed until I became 15 years old.

"I had one brother, Johnny Wolf; he was older than I was. He left me in 1985. He had lung cancer. I have some of the things he made and he wore. He was very special. We were very close. He was older, and I highly respected him. I tell everybody he was my mother, he was my father, he was my brother, he was my friend. He was everything to me. He taught me how to ride the bucking stock, and we would train horses for other people.

"We were on the rodeo circuit as bull riders. We rodeoed in 27 states, and then when I got all banged up and bruised up, I quit rodeoing. I was 35 years old. It means a great

deal to me. We wanted to be champion bull riders. It was an experience that I do believe if I could go back in time, I'd just do the same all over again. I didn't get rich, I didn't get killed, but it was a life that I really enjoyed. I would have loved to have gotten good enough to have a hat or boot named after me.

"It was a real exciting life, and I've tried to keep our lifestyle going. I'm still doing what I figure he would like me to do, keeping up our image and working with our people. Back then, I was also training trick animals for the rodeo circuit, and I got into using my animals in different things, like doing school talks. But my big love is doing Native American Powwows. For the last eight or nine years that's all I did, powwows and going to school and doing talks.

"Besides training animals, I'm also a professional knife thrower. I do knife shows where I throw knives. I have a lady who works with me a lot, and she'll stand up beside the board, and I'll surround her in what we call the blade of steel. Then I show the boys and girls that there's a difference in throwing a knife and controlling

LOUIE PLANT
FLATHEAD

"IF I DANCE WELL, THEN SOMEONE WILL SAY, 'HE PRAYS WELL.'"

Fifteen-year-old Louie Plant is a whirl of feathers and color as he performs the intricate steps of the Fancy Dance. The Fancy Dance generally attracts younger dancers because of its lively movement. The War Dance, the Round Dance, and the Snake Dance were also popular among the Flathead people. Louie's regalia is brightly colored blues, purples, and reds, with a large eagle in the center. He wears two bustles on the back and carries dance sticks. "I've been dancing just about all my life. My brother taught me to dance. He is a Fancy dancer, too. My mother did the beadwork on my regalia. She made all but the bustles—my dad made the bustles for me. Dancing is a prayer. The first dance is always a prayer. If I dance well, then someone will say, 'He prays well.'"

Ruben Salvador Cojo
Mescalero Apache Cheyenne

"I try to do my best to represent my family, to show people we are not all gone. We are still here."

The Apache are well known in history and legend, especially from the stories of their famous chiefs — Cochise and Geronimo. The Mescalero are one of several tribes of Apache. Ruben Cojo grew up on the Mescalero Apache reservation in New Mexico until he was seven years old.

"The Mescalero Apache reservation is next to White Sands, a real pretty country. The Apache learned how to live out in the desert. Their survival tactics had to do with their environment, their surroundings. For example, Mescalero Apache don't wear regular moccasins; they have little tabs at the toe of their moccasins, 'cause when they were in the desert they used those tabs to kick the cactus over.

"One of our state birds is like a blessing out there. In fact, it's pretty rare that you'd go out and see a bird like the roadrunner. It's a good-spirited bird. A roadrunner can kill a rattlesnake. They are pretty small birds, but they are fast.

"My dad is full-blooded Mescalaro Apache. A lot of the bloodline on that side of the Apache comes from Cochise. My mom is Cheyenne.

"The Mescalero Apache don't do their tribal dances out in a circle. In a lot of them you dance back and forth, back and forth. What you are doing is massaging Mother Earth. It's a graceful dance, and it's a dance that you can do solo, you can do it standing next to a person, or you can do it clenching elbows, your arms together, dancing back and forth. A lot of our dances are ceremonial dances.

"At powwows I do the Men's Northern Traditional Dance. A lot of my regalia, a lot of my representation is Men's Northern Traditional, but my colors — the black, the white, the yellow — are pretty much Apache. The yellow indicates the corn pollen that we use. It's one of the special things we use amongst our people.

"Parts of my regalia are made from buckskin and parts are made from cloth. It's got ribbon work. Everything is handmade. Everything is a representation of my life — my family, my tribe, my people, and who I'm with now. I have redtail hawk feathers and also eagle feathers. The redtail hawk feathers were given to me by my dad and my grandpa until I could earn my eagle feathers. A lot of

Mandala

my regalia represents those people who helped me. It helps me remember them no matter where they are. My regalia grows as I grow; things change on it through the years.

"My grandpa gave me my face paint. It represented the North for him — the things that he had seen and the trail he had seen in the North. That's what the two lines on my face mean. I chose white because of the snow in the North.

"I was born in the Southwest, but I was raised in the North. My stepfather is Chippewa, and that's why we grew up in those areas. We grew up among the Ojibwa and the Chippewa, and we learned a lot of their ways. I've been a lot of places, to Alaska and a lot of Canada and Mexico. Most of the traveling I've been doing is to see family.

"My wish for my people is to keep our traditions alive, to keep our dancing alive. Don't let it die. Teach the young ones what you can. I've encouraged and helped guys younger than me. Show people you are proud of who you are. I have a daughter who is only a year and four months. She is learning how to walk and dance.

"I'm out there because I'm proud of who I am. I try to do my best to represent my family, and show people we are not all gone. We are still here. I'm trying to pick up my language, too. Our language is still spoken on the reservation. A lot of my family are medicine people, spirited people, sticking with the culture. A lot of them still have it going stronger than ever. They speak Apache; they go through all the ceremonies. They do it all the way their ancestors and parents and grandparents were brought up. To an extent I am trying to live a traditional life."

AILEEN FOX-PLANT
OJIBWA OTTAWA

"I ALWAYS SAY, BE PROUD OF WHO YOU ARE — STAND TALL."

Aileen Fox-Plant is Ojibwa and Ottawa, both Woodland tribes. These two tribes, along with the Potawatomi tribe, are known as the Three Fires Confederacy. Aileen is at the powwow with her family — her husband, who is Flathead, and her two children, David, who just turned three, and the youngest, Albert Plant III, who is almost one.

"I'm teaching my children to dance. It's a family thing. I've been dancing for about 20 years. I've been a Jingle Dress dancer for about six years. Before, I was a Fancy Shawl dancer, and before that, I was a Traditional dancer. I made my regalia. The jingle cones are from the lids of Steve Eagle tins, but many people use Copenhagen tins. I did all the beadwork myself.

"I'm from Manitolan Island, Ontario, Canada. The reserve I'm from is called Bay of the Beavers. My Ojibwa language is important. It is part of who we are as Ojibwa people. I'm trying hard to talk to my kids in Ojibwa. To me, being Indian, Ojibwa, is to be a good Christian — to respect, to share, to love, to be strong. We're alcohol- and drug-free.

"My people were fishermen and trappers, and when the Jesuits came, they learned farming techniques. My great-great-grandfather, he was Potawatomi. My great-grandfather was a fisherman. That's how he survived. My grandfather is still a fisherman and hunter and farmer. My people are pretty easy going. I always say, be proud of who you are, stand tall."

Aileen's purse

101

MATT ADKINS
CHICKAHOMINY

" I WEAR THE BELLS TO LET THE CREATOR KNOW THAT I AM HERE."

Matt Adkins is the son of James "Redblood" Adkins. I met Matt about the same time that I met his father, and I was struck by the close bond between them. Matt is a Fancy dancer. And, thanks to his father, he is very knowledgeable in the traditions of his people.

"I'm with the Chickahominy tribe in Virginia. During the 1800s, they moved half of our tribe on the Trail of Tears to Oklahoma. During the Civil War we went to Canada to live with the Ojibwa in Kings Creek.

"I'm a Fancy dancer, and these bustles were given to me. I wear two bustles with brightly colored feathers. They are turkey feathers with chicken hackles on the tops. I have started patterns with mirrors in the center to reflect the sunlight. I made my beadwork. In the design, light blue represents the sky, the dark blue is the water. As you go in, the design goes into the Earth to the core. It symbolizes the Earth.

"My arm bustles are in the circle position to symbolize the world. My roach has deer hair and porcupine hair and beaded sockets. I wear hawk feathers in my roach because I don't have eagle feathers yet. In the old days they would roach their hair like a flattop is today, but they did it with bear grease to hold it up until it dried. After a while they started using porcupine and deer hair; it simulates roaching your hair.

"I wear a head band. My moccasins are buckskin. They have the same design as my cuffs. I wear the bells to let the Creator know that I am here. These are wands, twirlers. They have fishing swivels and then hackles that match my bustles, so that when I'm dancing I twirl them real fast.

"The Fancy Dance didn't start until the 1920s in Oklahoma on the Ponca Indian reservation. And the Poncas composed most of the old Fancy Dance songs. It's a quick and fancy dance, a competition dance, a quicker, faster movement, to show endurance. I used to be a Traditional dancer. I am 14 now, and I started dancing Traditional when I was nine months old. I've only been dancing Fancy Dance for a short time."

JERRY WARD
COMANCHE

"YOU DANCE FOR PEOPLE WHO CAN'T DANCE . . .
TO SHOW THEM YOU ARE THINKING ABOUT THEM, AND
TO CARRY ON THE TRADITION THAT HAS BEEN GOING
ON FOR HUNDREDS AND HUNDREDS OF YEARS."

Jerry Ward is very proud of his culture and knows a great deal about his people; he enjoys teaching others about the Comanche. He dances the Southern Straight Dance, also known as the Gentlemen's Dance.

"The Southern Straight Dance or Gentlemen's Dance was given to the Comanches by the Poncas in the 1930s and '40s. It had been given to them previously but they lost it. It started with the Poncas, and they gave it to other tribes. I'm a member of the Comanche War Dance Society. We have a dance every year back in Oklahoma, and that's the ceremonial dance that we do. It's the Helushka, the Ponca Straight Dance.

"It's a dignified slower-moving dance, real elegant. The significance is that it's a ceremonial dance, a war dance. Usually someone would announce that there was going to be a war excursion or war party, and they would have a feast or gathering of the people, and they would sing and dance all night. In the early morning they would slip away from the camp and meet at a prearranged site and then go on to their destination.

"I made my regalia. The feathers I wear are golden eagle and bluejay. I wear a golden eagle in my roach, and I have two center tail feathers that my grandfather loaned to me that came from a canyon down in Texas where the Comanches used to go and spend their winters. The bluejays I like to wear because they are like sentries out in the woods. If you are trying to sneak around and you make noise, they will call out and alert all the other animals.

"On my roach there's an ornament tied to the back of the feather called a roach feather ornament. It's made of horsehair and porcupine quills. It's something that I wear, and a lot of people nowadays don't. It's something I learned from my grandfather. At one time this decoration was similar to a military medal, awarded to someone after a certain feat in battle or a show of courage or something. The bluejay feather, it's a roach pin, and it's what holds my roach on. There's a pin on my scarf shaped like a starburst.

"The scarf is black. It represents the missionaries who came through Comanche country saying, 'Change your ways; the lifestyle you are living is evil, and you are not living according to God.' And, of course, the Comanches

Eagle feather bustle

"I carry a golden eagle flat fan, and in the other hand I carry a mirror board, a piece of wood with a mirror mounted onto the wood. It was an item introduced by the early traders, French, and early explorers. They brought trade items with them such as silver, mirrors, and beads, and the mirror fascinated the Indian people because they thought it was real magical and had a lot of power associated with that — being able to see yourself in a reflection like that. After the mirror became more customary, they used it to signal each other from a great distance. So they would melt these mirrors to the board to help keep them from breaking. Nowadays a lot of dancers use a stick instead of a mirror board — a stick that's beaded and decorated, called a coup stick. It's a French word meaning 'to strike.'

"I wear moccasins that have long fringe hanging down the back about seven or eight inches. This was designed so that when you lifted your foot up, then the fringe would cover your tracks up. The Comanches were among the first people to get the horse from contact with the Spaniards. So, typically, their clothing had more fringe than other Indians in the area.

"Sometimes I wear a little face paint at the corner of my eyes. A lot of people painted their eyes; they felt it helped them to see better. They felt the paint had power or medicine in it. They would have a vision quest, and that would determine the amount they painted their faces. Sometimes I vary my face paint a bit.

"I was always told that you dance for people who can't dance. You dance for them, to show them you are thinking about them, and to carry on the tradition that has been going on for hundreds and hundreds of years. A lot of places have contest powwows, and you are judged on how you dance in your area. That's drawing a lot of people into the powwow world. But the powwow started off as a social gathering, a time to bring food and sit and visit their families.

"When I'm not dancing, I'm doing my craftwork. My grandmother is a ribbonworker. She does Osage-style ribbonwork, Straight Dance clothes, and blankets. When I was younger, a lot of people did craftwork. But they only did one specific type, like beadwork, featherwork, or silverwork, and they stayed in that specific area. I've noticed that it kind of limited what you could do. So I set out to learn everything I could do. I make things for other dancers, things to decorate homes — this keeps my tradition alive.

"I feel that a lot of younger people nowadays back in Oklahoma are steering away from that. They choose to party and stray away from the traditions that have been handed

had been living that way for thousands of years, so they took that black color that the missionaries were wearing, and they made scarves and said, 'We are going to use this for something good, for how we believe.'

"The pin, it comes from a Mexican spur rowel, the round part of the spurs. The Mexicans, they like to use pointed ones, and cowboys in Texas and North America liked to use rounded-off spur jacks. The Comanches, they got those spur rowels from the Mexicans that they met in battle, so they made those scarf slides out of them.

"The breast plate is also Comanche. I spent a lot of hours researching, talking to tribal elders finding out not only what each piece was but how it evolved. The breast plate is made out of bones and glass beads and leather, and it's short; it only comes to the bottom of my solar plexus. The reason for that is the Comanche spent a lot of time on horseback, so they couldn't wear a long breastplate. It also protected the vital organs.

down. That's why a lot of Indian people turn to alcoholism for escape. There are not a lot of options. There's poverty. It's hard for Indians to get a job. We really weren't barbarians, painted savages, gathered around a campfire. We have our own customs, laws, beliefs that we passed down. When it comes down to it, we really weren't all that different.

"The Comanches were one of a kind. At one time the Comanches were an offshoot of the Shoshone. The story on how they came to split was told to me. There were boys playing a game 'called kick each other in the stomach until you fall down.' It was a way of providing them endurance for the life that they would have to live. But for them it was just a game. And one boy was kicked so hard in the stomach that he died from the blow,

and this fractured the tribe. One part of the tribe said: we should move away from this place because this is a bad thing that has happened here; one of our young boys lost his life. And the other part of the tribe said: it was an accident, and this is the type of life we lead. And so part of the ones that left traveled south into Texas and Kansas, and they became the Comanches.

"A lot of younger people are joining into the powwow world, and they want to get out there and dance and have a good time like everyone else. They are calling on other tribes' dances to do that. It's good to do those dances, but at the same time, you need to go with your own culture, to learn about what you are doing, to dance your own dance. Dancing has got to be more than a competition."

DAVE BALD EAGLE
LAKOTA

"WE SHOULD ALL LIVE TOGETHER AS ONE AND TRY TO PROTECT NATURE, BECAUSE EVERYTHING HAS BEEN PLACED ON EARTH FOR A REASON."

It was an extremely hot day at the powwow on Raccoon Mountain just outside Chattanooga, Tennessee. I wondered how the dancers could stand the heat, dressed in full regalia, when I noticed Dave Bald Eagle wearing an impressive war bonnet. Dave is an elder, a teacher, a spiritual advisor. He travels to powwows and dances and emcees. He is a member of the Lakota tribe of the Cheyenne River Lakota Nation.

"The war bonnet was presented to me by the Northern Cheyenne tribe at a ceremony in Montana, when they made me an honorary member of their tribe. They told me to wear this, to be proud to wear this at any appearances I make. Sometimes at dedications or honoraries or namings, I wear the war bonnet. I travel all over the world. I've been to Germany, France, China, Japan, and all over the country coast to coast. I'm here today in Chattanooga. This is my third year here.

"I've been traveling powwows since the '40s. I was two times national champion Fancy dancer. I started dancing right after the war, but when I was a kid,

about seven, eight, or nine, I was dancing then. After the war I started dancing again, and I'm still dancing today.

"The darker color of the war bonnet represents the Cheyenne, and the lighter color is the Lakota. We don't like the 'Sioux' word. We don't use that name. There are three dialects — Nakota, Dakota, and Lakota. The language is no different. It's just the starting of the word is a little different.

"I was born on the reservation along the Cherry Creek at Cherry Creek village just across the river from the community. I was born in a teepee back in 1919. At that time they didn't rush mothers to the hospital like they do nowadays. My parents are full-blood Lakota. Both my grandfathers and grandmothers taught me from the time I can't remember until I was 12 years old. I didn't go to school until then. But in between that time they drilled the culture, traditions, and history into me. One of my grandfathers, White Bull, was in the battle of Little Big Horn, and he told me all about it. From start to finish. I have it written down.

Eagle feather headpiece

"My first wife was a Lakota full-blood, and we have Lakota children from the same reservation. Also, later in years, I married a Belgian girl, and we have children that are half Lakota. Everything we do is passed on to them. I have 17 children all told. I've got about 28 or 29 grandchildren and four great-great-grandchildren. We had a family reunion, and over 200 were there. I have the responsibility of my children on different sides. My ex-wife has the full-blood kids, and my present wife is friends with my ex-wife. And we all work together as one big family. My children and grandchildren seek my advice. My grandchildren love to hear my stories.

"I got my name because the government translated my grandfather's name as Bald Eagle, so that's how we started. There were Little Bald Eagles and then Bald Eagle Bear, and ours was really Beautiful Bald Eagle. The eagle is very important to our tribe. The wearing of the eagle feather is very important. If a person drops an eagle feather, they have to have a ceremony before it is returned back to him. The ceremony is a prayer.

"The Lakota people are traditional, and still today they carry on the traditional ways of life. And the language is coming back pretty strong, and so is the buffalo within the reservations. All the Lakota, Nakota, and Dakota people are raising buffalo; they are bringing the buffalo back. The reservations are in South Dakota, North Dakota, Minnesota, Nebraska, Wyoming,

Porcupine and deer hair roach

Montana, and southern parts of Canada. The Lakota nation is one of the largest nations.

"Our culture and traditions relate to nature and wildlife. We are good with livestock, not very good at farming. We have clans. My clan is the Crazy Horse Descendency Clan.

"The Lakota have always been kind people. We invite people so much that we have people from Germany, Sweden, France, Italy, and all over come and visit our place in the summertime. We have guests constantly from foreign countries and from other tribes.

"I travel all over speaking about our culture, our traditional ways of life, and nature in particular. How we live with nature and learn from nature, and how we lived with nature in the past. I speak the Lakota language and teach it also. My parents spoke Lakota when I grew up. I am a teacher of language and history in all grades, from Head Start to big communities.

"I hope that I always travel around the world advising people on peace and unity and friendship, working for a better relationship between the American Indians and the people of the world. That is what I'd like to see in the future. We all live together. We all really need to teach what nature is here for. Every insect, every animal, every reptile, underwater, above water, in the air, and everyplace, we are all related together. And all the people, no matter what nationality, we should all live together as one and try to protect nature, because everything has been placed on earth for a reason."

DANIEL TRAMPER
EASTERN BAND CHEROKEE

"THE YOUNGER GENERATION,
THEY NEED TO HOLD ON TO THEIR OWN CULTURE . . .
BECAUSE THEY ARE THE FUTURE."

I always try to arrive at a powwow early enough to see the Grand Entry. That's when a special song is sung and all the dancers enter the ring for the first time. Part of what makes it so special is the opportunity to see the dancers' regalia, each one unique, special. Daniel Tramper caught my eye because of his Fancy Dance regalia, which is a profusion of bright pink and white feathers.

"I dyed the feathers myself; they are turkey spikes. The white hackles on there are rooster hackles. I have a bridge cloth and yoke with a white snow leopard in the middle. I carry a wand in each hand. It gives me rhythm, something to hang on to, and they twirl. I made pompoms for the ends with beads. They help me keep the rhythm of beat. I wear a roach out of porcupine guard hair and deer tail, and I've got two rocker feathers — some people call them honor feathers. A rocker is a see-saw type thing that keeps in beat with the music.

"I wear moccasins on my feet. They are handmade, made out of moose hide. I wear a scarf around my neck. A lot of dancers wear the chokers, but I wear a scarf. I chose it because I have a lot of things around my neck, and it keeps them tucked in so they don't hit my face when I'm dancing.

"I've been dancing about 23 years, ever since I was a little fellow. My father taught me to dance. He was a Fancy dancer, too. He still dances every now and then. A friend of his out of Oklahoma taught him to dance. Back then it was more making a living for your family by doing shows on the street. I started out when I was young doing shows and traveling, and I started competing about seven years ago.

"I've always lived on the reservation. I know a little of the Cherokee language. My mom speaks pretty good Cherokee, but she doesn't speak it that often. Our language is dying out here. I need to learn it myself.

"I'm involved with kids right now that I teach every Wednesday. I'm teaching powwow-type dancing. I've been teaching them about seven or eight months. A mother on the ceremonial grounds asked me if I'd teach it and said that she'd pay me for my time, but I was always taught that the dance was given to me and I have no right to charge

Pottery

anybody. That's one way I have of giving back what was given to me.

"I'm getting some of my elders to come down and teach our own traditional dancing. We started that last week, and it seemed to catch on. Some of our dances are the Green Corn Dance, which was like a prayer dance, giving thanks for having a good harvest, or praying to have a good harvest; the Beaver Dance; the Quail Dance; the Horse Dance; and a Friendship Dance. A way long time ago, they called it the Six Nations Dance 'cause some of the six nations came down and we got together, and then it became a Friendship Dance.

"A Quail Dance is like, if you've ever seen a family of quails when they run up on something, they'll back up and then go around it; they don't ever try to go over it, and that's what this dance represents. The dancers go up, back up, spread out. You have two lines, a man's line and a woman's line. Then the women go one way and the men

the other, and then they all scatter into the woods like a family of quail would. It's an old dance passed down generation by generation.

"Our Beaver Dance shows how we used to go out looking for Beaver. They have simulated Beaver and a group of people in a circle, and they do their songs. Some of the songs say a lot of words, and some are just syllables. The Horse Dance was mimicking the horse. We were grateful for the Europeans' bringing the horse over. Our people were mostly farmers, and we used the horse for that.

"We never did the powwow-type dancing. Ours were more prayer dances. We still hold our Stomp Dances here every third weekend of the month. And some of our old dances we are bringing back, trying to keep our traditions going. A Stomp Dance is just the Cherokee way of saying 'it's our dancing.' We go out there and sing songs that represent different things. There has been a revival of dancing on the reservation because our kids are losing interest in it. What I figure is, teach the kids what they want to learn, and then bring our own dancing in with it, so they'll learn their own. I figure you got to know who you are before you can start doing somebody else's dances.

"I have a son, and I've taught him. I was dancing at a powwow when he was right at two years old, and he got out there and walked around with me. And the next powwow we made him a little outfit and he took off, and he's been going ever since. He'll be nine in February. His name is Scrappy.

"You see how bright colored Fancy dancers are; they are the most flamboyant dancers out there. One of the stories about them is that they are mimicking a horse, how a young horse would run around and strut around and prance around and jump and kick. Like a Tennessee Walker struts and walks — that's how a Fancy dancer is. They want to be noticed, for everybody to see them. The Fancy Dance is a western Plains dance. There are two types of dancing, northern and southern. Southern starts out slow and gets fast. The northern stays the same speed and has more acrobatics. Southern is more straight type with more footwork.

"The way I was taught to dance is like the rabbit dances. That's where you take your two index fingers and stick them up to your head and hop around like a little rabbit. It was to get you in time to the drum. Once you learn the beat of the drum, that's where the steps come in. Most of our dances represent something of nature.

That's fun for the little ones. You can get the little ones to do a lot of things if you make it fun for them. That's the way I got started, and that's how I try to teach the kids here, but the older ones don't want to do that.

"Growing up on the reservation was a good time. I grew up doing shows a lot. I was always out there among the public. It's always been neat to me. When I was little, when we'd go on trips I thought that was great. In summer we were always in Cherokee doing shows. The powwow circuit was really out west then; powwows here are really just getting started good, just in the past 10 years. Now there's powwows everywhere. I go pretty much in the summertime. We slow down in the wintertime. We try to hit at least one a month.

"What we had a long time ago was our festival with the powwow in it. The fall festival last year was the 83rd, a combination of carnival, stick ball games, dances, different types of food, kind of like a state fair. It's held every October.

"Stick ball is how we used to settle our disputes. Like one community had a rivalry with another community, and they'd play for two or three days at a time. You go to a score of 12, and it's got a little of everything combined in it. I played it as a kid. You have two sticks you carry to pick up the ball, but once you get the ball picked up in the stick, you can reach in and carry it in your hand. A long time ago they'd use the sticks to trip you up.

"We had some pretty good games here. One time the Chocktaws came up and they wanted to play us, and they didn't realize how rough it was. They've never been back. So it's now mainly Cherokee against Cherokee. Some other tribes play it in a different way, but the Cherokee originated stick ball.

"We've always been friendly people, always humorous, joking around. We never really turned anybody away from our tribe. We have 11,000 Indians on the reservation. We were the ones that stayed here because of Tsali.

"On the day after Thanksgiving is a holiday on the reservation we call Tsali day. He is a hero here. He gave his life up so we could stay here. This year the little group I work with, we got together and we had our first annual Tsali Day, and we had our princesses, chief, and elders. We are going to try to do it every year.

"We are working on Project Healthy Cherokee, and we're trying to get a lot of things going for kids here. We have an alcohol problem on the reservation. We're

trying to get our kids interested in something else other than that. A lot of people work off the reservation because they can make more money. But they say you can take the fellow away from the Cherokee, but you can't take the Cherokee away from the fellow. I work for the Cherokee Boys Club. It's a good job if you want to work at home. We've got our casino started here, and that gave a lot more jobs.

"The younger generation, they need to hold on to their own culture, no matter what culture they are, because they are the future. They are going to be our leaders one day, and we are not always going to be here to teach them. They need to learn their own culture no matter what they are — Indian, Mexican, or Black. But a lot of youth don't care anymore; they just want to do what they see on TV, no matter what.

"We get a lot of kids here who want to learn who are not Cherokee, and I was always taught you don't turn a kid away, no matter who he is."

supposed to be at the arch of your foot, not beyond the other foot — little baby steps. The women used to take the shawl when the men went out to war or fighting and cover them when they came back to heal them. The beads add color to the fringe on my dress. We both wear eagle plumes.

"It didn't used to be okay for women to wear eagle feathers or dance in the ring, but now they can. Women could stand on the side but not in the middle of the arena. It's just our generation that's trying to be strong. Our people don't voice themselves like Black people do. Indians were shunned, so they were afraid that something bad would happen.

Beaded deerskin pouch

Michigan have been dancing all their lives So I just started dancing. "

Sharon wears a white buckskin dress with long fringe. "I got the buckskin for my regalia. The colors that I chose for my dress are the Chippewa colors—blue, pink, white, black. The fringe moves when the traditional women dance since there is not much else that moves. I used to have a more traditional outfit when I was younger, but I always wanted a white buckskin.

"You have different types of Traditional dancing — Southern Traditional and Northern Traditional. I dance Northern Traditional. The southern women tend to bow at certain honor beats of the drum. They bow to the earth. Traditional women hold their fans up and sway them, and some hold them to the side. Some of the Northern Traditional stand in place and dance. It's your choice.

"The Fancy Shawl dancers are faster. Traditional are slow dances. We don't take big steps. Your toes are always

"People used to make fun of Indians, but now it's different. I'm allowed to be proud; we can be proud of ourselves. I hope my children carry on their traditions. They should never die. I have four boys, three who are dancing."

Diane's oldest son makes crafts — bracelets and pouches. "I know he'll carry on our traditions. It's hard for the young people. We have the highest rate of suicide in teenagers because they are so confused. They don't know which way to be. One Indian man said we have to quit fighting among ourselves and be one people. Each nation has its own ways of doing things. We should come together as one people to voice for all of us what we want. We are supposed to have a national powwow, but a lot of Indians are still hiding. It's sad we have to be that way.

"I wish that our people would come out a little more. The Native Americans were here; they have been here. In history they teach children that Columbus discovered America. The Native Americans were here before. It was already discovered. The history books are wrong. We discovered it. Also, it was the French who started scalping, and then blamed it on the Indians. The Indians only mocked them and did it back.

"Something should be done for the Native Americans. Clinton said that he was going to try to get a Native American day — one day that we can gather together and

be one — but he hasn't done it yet. The government needs to go back and rewrite history; these children are learning the wrong way. It's hard when little children come and look at you like you're different, like, are you really Indian? They don't know. I never thought about it till I started dancing. My brother would wear a black arm band on Columbus Day.

"Native Americans are about Mother Earth. We have one thing we believe in; that is the Creator. We respect and acknowledge Mother Earth. Mother Earth provides us with everything — trees, plants, animals — and we take care of Mother Earth. For example, trees have spirits. When you cut one down, you are supposed to lay some tobacco and pray for that tree.

"Tobacco is a spiritual thing. We use it in our ceremonies. We use sage, cedar, and honey. We crumble tobacco and drop it on the ground. We offer something for the life; we offer tobacco. We are saying, thank you for letting us have it. In Canada they have a lot of tobacco fields. The Indians grew tobacco. Mother Earth gave it to us.

"Native Americans have big hearts. They make sure their family is taken care of."

Loom

121

JAVIER ALARCON
AZTEC

"BEFORE THE SPANISH THE REGALIA WOULD HAVE BEEN PURE GOLD, BUT NOW IT IS PAINTED."

I admired Javier Alarcon's majestic dancing at many powwows before I gained an interview with him. He has so many exquisite dances — the Eagle, the Sun, the Emperor — and in each he wears headpieces which make him appear to be eight feet tall. His dances require great stamina; he twirls, leaps, stomps, and hurtles high into the air, with the grace of an animal, a bird. He is hard to approach at a powwow because after he leaves the dance arena, he is immediately surrounded by children and adults who want to talk to him, take photographs of him, just look at him in his splendid regalia.

"I made all my regalia. I did research at the Museum of Anthropology in Mexico about clothes, dance, and music. My mother's people are Aztec, and my father's side is mixed with Spanish. His grandfather is the only one mixed with Spanish blood; all the other family members are Aztec."

Javier is resplendent in his regalia of gold and silver, red and blue, set with stones and beads accompanied by masses of plumes and feathers. "On my eagle headdress, the feathers are pheasant. I also use rooster feathers. They are a mark of rank. In the old days the plumes would have been only eagle feathers, but in Mexico the eagle is protected. Out of respect I don't use them. The eagle of Mexico is the royal eagle or golden eagle. My headdress represents the golden eagle. The turquoise stones represent purity; the color represents a very esteemed warrior.

"My regalia represents the last emperor of Mexico. It's a fallen eagle. He's the one who fought with Cortez when Cortez landed in Mexico. This regalia is official. Before the Spanish the regalia would have been pure gold, but now it is painted. Cortez, when he returned to Europe, reported that what he had seen in Mexico was much more lavish than anything he had seen in the courts of Europe. There were Aztecs whose business was scouting for feathers — grading them, cataloging them — and they had a warehouse for feathers.

"Aztec culture was imperial. They had schools for dancing, singing, astrology. To know the culture of Mexico, you have to know all of the things of astrology. They were very accomplished. It's not easy to understand the

culture. For example, the Aztec used human sacrifice. On the other hand, the Spanish were cannibals, yet they said that the Aztec were cannibals. Also, Aztecs would put on medicines to scar the skin in patterns. They would also paint their skins.

"The Eagle Dance was special. When you are a warrior, you can use the eagle feather. If you were not a good warrior, you could not use it. They prepared for religion also with the Eagle Dance. The king could use the Ketzel feathers only. You have to earn the right to use eagle feathers.

"The Sun Dance is for the Maya culture — performed when the sun is really strong. The face paint represents musical notes. We use a special fruit in Mexico to make rattles for the legs. The jewelry I use is gold material. Originally, the jewelry was made of gold and jewels.

"My culture wants respect. The people come here [to the U.S.] because in Mexico there is no work. I just want respect for my brothers in Mexico."

Kristen and Chipa Wolf with Javier Alarcon

REUBEN JESS SANDOVAL, JR.
YAKIMA

"I DANCE FOR MY FAMILY."

"I've been dancing for 15 years. I'm 18 now, so I've been dancing since I was three. It was the way I was raised. My family would always take me to powwows. I got the feel for it, and I've been doing it ever since. I went mostly to local powwows until I was 16, then I started going up into Canada and down into Oregon, started traveling around. Out here, this is the way I pay my bills. I enjoy doing it. It keeps my culture alive.

"Yakimas were a peaceful tribe until the white settlers came out. They didn't respect our ways, and that's what started wars. Yakimas, if they have a problem, would gamble or talk it out, and that's how they would settle things. A lot of people have the illusion that all tribes were savages, which isn't true. If they got pushed to the limit, they were going to stand up for what they believe in.

"We were mostly hunters and fishermen. During fishing season, we'd go down to the Columbia river and fish for salmon; we'd hunt for deer and elk; we'd pick roots up in the mountains. We didn't farm until we were put on a reservation. The reservation covers a good majority of Washington State. The last I heard, we had 5,000 enrolled members in my tribe aged 18 and over, so that wasn't really counting the younger kids — there are probably about 8,000 enrolled members.

"I'm a Grass dancer and a Traditional dancer, so I know how to dance two different styles. My regalia is Grass Dance. The Grass Dance is the old style of dancing. There are about four or five different stories that go with it. The story I'm most familiar with is that a long time ago, before the Northern Plains tribes would set up a camp, they would call out their grass dancers. The grass dancers would dance down all the grass and bless the ground at the same time. Dancing down the grass would make it easier for people to walk around, to put up their teepees. Also, blessing the ground was so nothing would happen to the people.

"One of my aunts made my regalia for me. An old choker that I have belonged to one of my great-uncles. It's made out of glass beads and bone. There's ribbon, yarn on my regalia. Light blue, black, and red are my favorite colors. Red will be in my next regalia. The roach is feathers from the bald eagle. The piece over my face is a scarf.

Kachina

abalone shell on the choker — we don't have a lot of it in Washington State.

"If I had the money to do it right now, I'd go back home to the reservation. It's the place I love. It can be hard there. Even though it's on the reservation, there is a lot of racism.

"In our religion we have what we call washat, a long house. It has dirt in the center where we dance during our services. We have seven drums, and they usually have seven men who are singing on those drums. And each man sings two songs, so you dance for 14 songs straight.

"For us, when we sweat at our services, it's kind of like saying confession. It's our way of sweating out our sins, showing the Creator that we are sorry for what we have done. Our people were stubborn and weren't so easy to give up our religion for Christianity. We had one of the best treaties of any of the tribes in the U.S. Those who want to, remain traditional and are learning the language, are learning the ways. We have one type of dance that we do for services. We have services before huckleberry season, for a salmon feast when the fishermen first come back from salmon fishing, and we have a salmon feast.

"If I was back home, it would be off-season. There is a powwow almost every weekend somewhere. Ninety-eight percent of the people at powwows at home are Indian. It's our thing. Other tribes come to our powwows but not many white people. It's open to everybody, but 98% are Indians.

"I'm a mixture of Yakima, Warm Springs, Nez Perce,

A lot of times if I wear paint, it's because I'm feeling down; I put on face paint, and for some reason it gives me that boost to keep going. I carry a fan made of eagle feathers. I wear moccasins, buckskin.

"When I dance, I dance for my family. Recently I had a couple of grandmothers that passed away, and when I dance, I dance for them. When I sweat, that's a way to show how much I care for them. My hair is almost always braided. I wear braid wraps or hair ties. On my choker I have two pieces of abalone shell with pieces of horse hair coming off it. Very seldom will you see

Winnepong, and Apache, but mostly Yakima. Yakima are mellow people. One old guy said when you get mad, what do you say? We say, We use your language, the white man's language, because there are no cuss words in our language.

"We are seeing fewer teen dancers at powwows. As things get more modern, they want to be like other teens. Gangs are becoming popular. A lot of the Yakima teenagers speak more Mexican than Yakima. There are more Mexicans than Yakimas on the reservation. Mexicans come to Washington State for hop harvesting. There are many Mexicans in the fields.

"My dad is really proud of me. When I was younger I used to tell my dad, I'm going to do nothing but dancing; that's the way I'm going to earn my living. He said that he hadn't seen that yet. It's a risk I'm willing to take. I've only been dancing Grass for four or five months.

"Yakimas are really nice, really loving. They'll take care of you if you treat them right. It kind of goes both ways. If you meet an Indian you think is bad, don't judge all of them by that. Don't judge one people by one person."

ERNEST DOCKERY
NORTHERN CHEYENNE

"WE FOUNDED THE SOCIETY AS A WAY OF PRESERVING THE HERITAGE AND TRADITION OF OUR PEOPLES."

At every powwow there is a veterans' ceremony or dance. Ernest Dockery is a founding member of the Native American Veterans Warrior Society.

"I grew up in Wyoming. I lived there till I was 17 and I went in the service. 'Walks Like A Bear' is my name my grandmother gave me when I was small. That's my tribal name."

At powwows Ernest wears a uniform adorned with the many medals he has earned. He proudly explained the meaning of them to me. "I was in the Army and the Air Force. I was in the Air Force first. I'm a master parachutist, jumpmaster. The blue one is Antarctic service (twice), Vietnam Service Medal (three times), Vietnam Campaign Medal, National Defense, Air Force Good Conduct, Army Good Conduct, Purple Heart (twice), Air Force Achievement, Army Commendation Medal with V for Valor, and Bronze Star (twice) with Valor. And, of course, my Combat Infantry Badge Second Award. This is a Presidential Unit Citation (three times), Outstanding Unit Citation (three times), and the Vietnam Cross of Gallantry.

I was a Platoon Sergeant, an E7. I was with the 75th Infantry Brigade First Ranger Battalion in Vietnam.

"My grandmother's uncle was Two Moon. He was a Cheyenne leader at the Battle of Little Big Horn. My grandmother was born in the cold after Sandcreek, the winter of 1865. Sandcreek was in 1864, what they call the Sandcreek Massacre. My grandmother was born the following winter. She was at the Little Horn. There were two rivers the Cheyenne called the Little Horn and the Big Horn and somehow it got mutilated into the Little Big Horn. But actually it's the Little Horn River, and that's where the Battle of the Greasy Grass took place — my grandmother was there.

"Growing up in Wyoming as a mixed-blood Native American was a pretty rough life, so my mother kept things to herself for a long time. I was in the service before I found out about my heritage, and I've been pursuing it ever since. Sometimes when you look into it, you run into a brick wall. My mother and my father passed away, and I don't have any uncles or aunts still alive. My mother had one cousin on the reservation 10 years ago,

131

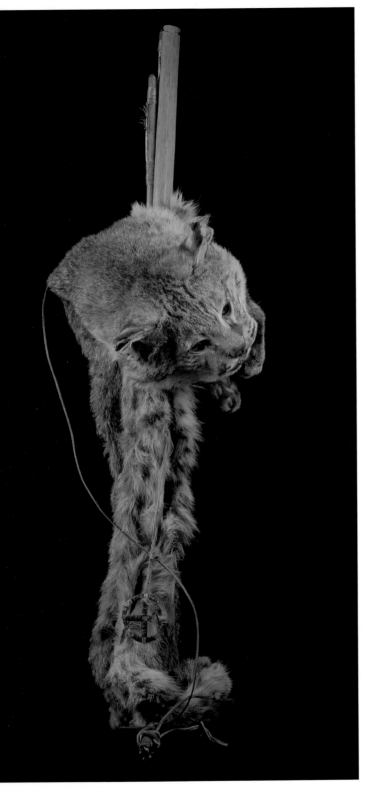

Bobcat bow and arrow quiver

along with Mr. Levi Walker, and several others too numerous to name. We founded the society as a way of preserving the heritage and tradition of our peoples. We are an education society. After all of our expenses come out, the rest goes into a scholarship fund for Native American children. We are strictly a not-for-profit organization, and we function totally on donations.

"My dance staff is wood wrapped with leather and wolf fur, and it's painted in the Vietnam Veteran colors. I have otter fur here and a golden eagle claw, a golden eagle feather and two hawk feathers that were given to me by different people. They honored me by giving me these feathers, so I put them on my dance staff. The Warrior Society, we use this staff as our eagle staff when we do color guards. I'm semi-retired, and when I come to the powwows, I do color guards. We are like a big family. These gatherings are almost like a family reunion.

"My choker is a piece that was worn by warriors to protect them from getting their throats cut in battle. It's part of their battle armor. This hair pipe is made from bison bone, and the vertical pieces in it are made from human rib over 100 years ago. This is some of the stuff that was given to me that had belonged to Two Moon.

"These were not choker spacers. I chose to make spacers out of them and to wear them to honor him 'cause these are some of the things he left. In the center is a bear tooth and bear fur of the Bear Clan. That's where I come in, Walks Like a Bear. I'm Bear Clan 'cause Two Moon was Bear Clan. We more or less go in the direction of the mother's heritage.

"One thing that I would like to say is that the past is past and we have to look forward to the future — whatever future there is for us, the way things are going now. I see progress coming way too fast, and the people can't keep up with it. We need to slow down, we need to stop. We need to smell the roses. We need to look at each other and realize that if we keep going in the direction we are going in now, we are going to push ourselves right out of existence. That is what I see.

"Powwows, they bind us together, they bring us together, they are all family, they are friends — no matter whether they are mixed-blood, full-blood or no Native American blood at all — they are all welcome here. They are all brothers and sisters. And we have to see things that way. We have to stop the racial slurs. We have to stop categorizing."

and he's not there anymore, and I don't have any idea where to find him.

"I'm the National Commander of the Native American Veterans Warrior Society. I am one of the founders of it,

TSANI TURNER
CHEROKEE LAKOTA

"IT'S FITTING THAT THE ONES WHO ACTUALLY
FOUGHT FOR THE COUNTRY, TO KEEP IT FREE,
WOULD NOW BE THE WARRIORS LEADING
IN THE WARRIORS DANCE."

I was introduced to Tsani Turner by Ernest Dockery. Tsani is a veteran, as well as the founder and editor of the *Cherokee Foothills* magazine.

"My name is Chali Wechetoga, which means Eagle Eye. I go by the name of Tsani which means John in Cherokee.

"My father, who is Cherokee, taught me. I grew up in Massachusetts. My father is from Arkansas. We are descendants of the Trail. When he met my mother, he moved to Massachusetts, and I moved out when I was 18, never to go back again. He taught me all about my heritage. He made me understand that I was Tsalagi, Cherokee. 'Tsalagi' is the word we use for Cherokee. He would fashion bows and arrows and take us in the woods to hunt. We would even go to powwows.

"I was in the U.S. Navy. The medals I've got are Overseas Combat, Overseas Deployment, National Defense, Vietnam Defense (three tours), and Vietnam Campaign ribbon. I have a six-strand choker which I made. The eagle on it is symbolic of Eagle Eye. My father always called me that ever since I was a little child. He'd drop something on the floor, and he'd say 'Eagle Eye.'

"This is medicine bag, a new medicine bag. Very sacred things are going in there. It's a reminder that you are one of the children of the Creator. Every time you bend over to get a drink, every time it touches your body, it's a reminder that you belong to the Creator, not to the other side. That's your medicine; it's a constant reminder. Just like a crucifix is to a Catholic. We honor our traditions, being native.

"This is my knife; I made it. It is deer hoof. These deer hooves for the most part come from deer raised and slaughtered on farms for meat. It's a belief by Native Americans to honor that animal by using everything you can. So it's an honor to this deer that I now take it into the ring. The gold braid is Tsalagi Warrior Society out of Quala Boundary in Cherokee, North Carolina. Quala Boundary is the boundary that is now the reservation; it was part of the treaty agreement.

"On my earring, the pipe signifies the love of peace. We don't call them peace pipes; they are sacred pipes, personal pipes. The quill is called 'magudi'; it gave the porcupine strength and in turn gives us strength. The rest are feathers and the turquoise rock. On my beret there's a

Hawk war shield

lot of veterans honored, pins that people have gifted me, and the great seal of the Cherokee nation. These are feathers honoring fallen brothers — palmia, hawk feather, painted eagle feather, and this is an eagle out of Africa — it is not endangered.

"I'm a member of the Native American Veterans Warrior Society. The front two men, my commander and the elder, one had a great-uncle and one had a grandfather that fought at the Little Big Horn. It was an honor for me to walk with these people in the ring of honor. We are basically a society of warriors of all the nations. It's fitting that the ones who actually fought for the country, to keep it free, would now be the warriors leading in the warriors dance.

"Native Americans were in communications during the war. I speak Cherokee, and I was in communications, top secret crypto. I was in and out of Danang three times, and on a ship that floated all the way down south. When I first went to Vietnam, they blew my barracks up. Welcome to Vietnam. When I flew into Danang, my helicopter was shot down, and I had to come to the realization at 19 years old that all they can do is kill me.

"Nixon was the only one who promised to take us out, and he did. The other ones just promised. That makes him better than the rest of them. Veterans have a special place in their hearts for Nixon."

Ruben "Kahoo" Burgess
Comanche

"THE DRUM IS THE HEARTBEAT OF OUR PEOPLE."

The drum is an essential part of the powwow. "Drum" not only refers to the instrument, but also to the group of singers that surround it. Each powwow usually has a lead drum as well as other drums who are invited. At many of the powwows we attended there was a drum competition. Ruben "Kahoo" Burgess is the lead singer for The Plainsmen.

"We are all singers. We try to get singing in harmony. The lead singer has to do it all. You have to set the tempo or atmosphere of the powwow. Certain songs go to different things, how you want to feel. There are different harmonies. If you want to feel strong, there are songs for it. If you want to feel like flying away, there are songs for that, too. It makes you think about a lot of things.

"We all sing in sync at the same time. A lot of drums limit people, but in Oklahoma it is an open drum as long as you can sing. You have the responsibility to learn. You have to obey the rules. You have to listen. You learn from that.

"When I was four years old, my grandpa took me out to the drum, and I started singing from there. I didn't really start singing serious until I was about 13 years old. Then I started leading songs, but not for a certain group. My uncle, R. C. Mowatt, is the drum keeper. He asked me to lead them and try to show the younger guys how I sing — the different ways of singing songs, where they come from, what they are about.

"At home in Oklahoma they still have drums that sit up on the site. There is a center drum. Most are handmade. Some northern groups use bass drums and softer sticks. Usually the head singer has his own drum.

"There are songs that we call straight songs — a good old straight song that's just melody, no words. It's like an oldie on the radio. There's a feeling that comes from it. Old people, if you watch, they feel it. You get a spirit off songs like that. You can tell an old song from a contemporary song. Other songs tell a story, like Veterans' songs, Honor songs, Flag songs — they have words that mean something.

"When I was born, my grandpa got a tape recorder and put it under my pillow and started playing Gourd Dance songs — since I was three days old. It just came naturally for me. Me and my cousin Charlotte, we grew up

together, and she always used to put a blanket on and dance, and I would turn the laundry basket over and start singing, and it shocked my family because I stayed in sync at a young age. It surprised my mom because at two years old I started singing a Gourd Dance song, and I sang it the way it's supposed to be sung. She went home and told my grandpa, and from there he said I would be a good singer.

"My uncle and I made the drum out of rawhide. We stretched it over a hull. The northern tribes like Cree and Bloods, they have a hand-drum, and they do a reverb with their fingers for love songs. But we use drumsticks — take a stick and wrap it up in buckskin. Nowadays we use fiber glass rods (fishing rods) and wrap them up. They are wrapped in angora or buckskin.

"There are different songs for different categories. Fancy Dance is a faster dance so you use a faster beat. The Traditional, you sing a strong song. It's mostly a north-

ern song. Me and my Uncle Victor, we practiced and learned how to sing northern songs, which are higher pitched, with different honor beats.

"The difference between southern singing and northern singing is in southern, every song will have a lead, which is the person who starts the song, and it has a second when everyone comes in and they repeat or finish what the lead singer started. In the middle there are three honor beats, three hard hits; then it repeats. In northern you don't have those three hard down-beats; one person does honor beats, four, five, or seven honor beats or down-beats.

"Drum groups now make tapes. They record and put their music on tapes and sell them. You can learn off that. Some groups don't want you to sing their songs. You have to get permission to sing them. We mostly stick to the songs that I made or ones we have the right to sing. I've composed about 23 or 24 songs on my own. Everybody has their own melody. I make some songs with words in them about my elders and about the birds, and some melodies, and a love song for my girlfriend. Some of my songs are spiritual. Sometimes you don't dance for you; you dance for those who can't dance anymore or couldn't dance. You dance and lift someone's spirits.

"The flute is for your own personal thing. You might play it for your family or loved ones. We might do it for show, but not along with powwow. In Oklahoma you either sing or dance. We can't wear our outfits when we sing. You change into street clothes. You can't wear shorts. It isn't respectful. Some things you don't question. There are certain rules. We don't eat or drink at the drum. An animal gave his life for the drum; you have to respect that. If you want to join in a drum, you ask permission to join in. Most will let you. I try to hand down my singing to those who want to learn. Powwows and singing are so spiritual it gives me chills. You sing and you sound good and you can feel it. There is something to it; I can't stay away from it. I think about my grandpa and grandma and other ones who have gone on; that's what I think about. It's a healing, it's

medicine for me. If kids want to learn, it's not easy. It takes a lot of work, a lot of practice, a lot of heart. The heart is where it is at. You have to be focused.

"The drum is the heartbeat of our people. No matter where you are, you can tell. In Oklahoma we put it in the center, because the heart is in the center of the body. The people dance around as opposed to on the side. This is a festival. There is no fire. In private we sing totally different songs. It's deep, more spiritual.

"I've been Grass dancing about a month. My regalia was handed down to me from my dad. R. C.'s wife, Bobbie, it was her son's, and she gave it to Cleeto, and he adopted me and gave it to me.

"I hope to let the younger generation know that maybe I can be a role model for them. I am thankful to the old people for teaching me, for showing me the ways. I'm trying to hold onto it. We all get confused with life in general. It's hard to stay on the red road, or powwow highway, or whatever you call it. It's not easy, this life. But it has its good points. I'd like to tell the elders thank you for showing me the way."

NEIL LAHR
BLACKFEET

"DANCING IS FUN."

Neil Lahr, 11 years old, is a Grass dancer from the Blackfeet tribe. Blackfeet were particularly known for their Sun Dance, as well as a ceremony known as the Horse Dance.

"I've been dancing for four years. I learned from watching people. My mom and dad made my regalia. I travel around to powwows in Canada and the Northwest. Dancing is fun."

LESLIE MORTON
SALISH PEND D'OREILLE

"I GO TO A LOT OF POWWOWS."

Nine-year-old Leslie Morton is a Jingle dancer. "I've been dancing for a year and a half. I just placed first in 7- to 12-year-old Jingle-dancing competition. Betty Morton made my regalia. She is a seamstress and has a shop. Jackie McDonald did my bead work. The fur on my hair is otter. I got it from my mom, who got it from her great-great-grandmother. My plumes were given to me by my sister, who taught me how to dance. I go to a lot of powwows."

JENNA SKUNKCAP
BLACKFEET

"I LEARNED TO DANCE ON MY OWN."

Jenna SkunkCap, seven years old, is Blackfeet, a Northern Plains tribe. At one time, they were known as one of the largest tribes of that region. Jenna is a Fancy Shawl dancer.

"I've been dancing since I was one year old. I learned to dance on my own. My mom did the beadwork on my outfit. My feather comes from an eagle. My little sister, Chenille, dances too."

YOLANDA RAE OLD DWARF
CROW

"I WANT TO BE A LEADER INSTEAD OF A FOLLOWER."

Yolanda Rae Old Dwarf is a very special 14-year-old. She follows the ways of her Crow people, and, thanks to her mom, Julie Old Dwarf, she is well versed in their traditions. Julie helped fill in the details as we talked. Yolanda is a good role model not only for her own people, but for all of our youth today. She cares about who she is; she is respectful of her elders. She touched my heart with her words and her wisdom.

"My nickname is Lani. I am a traditional Crow dancer. I'm dressed the traditional old way with an elk tooth dress with a silk under-dress. The elk teeth are ceramic. I wear a traditional headband that's about a finger's width from the top of my hairline and down over the sides of my head. The braids are started at the tips of my ears so that just the tips of my ears show — that's traditional Crow. I have mink fur wrappings on the ends of my hair to lengthen it."

"She carries a fan that she also carries into the Peyote meetings for the Native American Church," Julie added. "She's also a Catholic, and she serves during Mass. Part of her outfit her grandmother gave her the right to wear. First her grandmother gave her the right to wear the eagle feather on the right side of her head. Then she gave her the elk teeth, and the color, and the style. Once she has them, she can pass them on four times for her children. Her grandma also gave her the right to wear money, and anytime she goes out to any kind of function, then they use that. When she wears money, it will bring her money.

"On the back she has the right to wear the muffler, which is the scarf traditionally worn over the head, but now they wear it draped over their shoulders. On the back she also has the white ermine, which is in the Crow way — part of the Tobacco Society which her grandma also introduced her to. On the back is a little stuffed, designed pouch; it can be any kind of design or color, and in it is her belly button. When she was born, we saved her belly button, and her grandma put it into the pouch. This is to make sure that when she grows up, she will be a mother, that she will carry on the traditions, and that she will see her grandchildren, also.

"She wears red paint straight out from the corner of her eyes. All Crow people can wear the red eye paint like that. They are known for it. She can wear it in a 'V' there, too. From her grandmother she has the right to bring in her water for her own Peyote meetings, for her own religion. And when they do that, they make a 'V' and color it in."

"I have the right to wear red on my forehead," Lani stated. "My grandmother wanted me to have all the rights because she knew I would cherish them and that I would understand them and pass them on."

Julie continued, "She carries her shawl while she dances. Sometimes they wear it over themselves, but with the elk tooth dress they usually carry it on the left side; on the right side she carries her fan. She has fully beaded top leggings and the moccasin bottoms. She has squash blossom turquoise jewelry and a ring that matches. That's pretty traditional. She wore a medallion earlier.

She has the belt strap on the right side, which means that she is single. The belt was her grandmother's. She passed away in 1990."

"Five years ago my hair was down to my waist, and I cut it to just below my ears when my grandmother died," Lani continued. "It's a Crow tradition."

Julie is very proud of her daughter. It shows in her eyes and in her voice. "When Lani was 12, she was one of eight Crow poets selected from the schools to go to Washington, D.C., to read their poetry in front of a standing-room-only audience at the Library of Congress."

"We were the first group of Native Americans to read there," Lani stated with pride. "I wrote 12 poems. I wrote a poem called 'Wise Woman' that was about my grandmother, Frances Gardner Old Dwarf. Part of what we did in Washington was go to the cemetery 60 years after Chief Plenty Coups went and gave his coup stick, staff, war bonnet, and flag to the Tomb of the Unknown Soldier. We read there. Chief Plenty Coups was the last chief of the Crow tribe. One of the kids who went with me was the Chief's great-great-great-grandson. Chief Plenty Coups adopted children; he never had any of his own."

Lani is very proud of her heritage. She's half Crow and an enrolled member of the tribe. Her father, Nathan, is Crow, the Piegan Clan. She's also one-fourth Norwegian and one-fourth German from her mother's side. "I'm proud of my mother. Even though she is not Indian, she is considered one. She has her own clan; she was adopted by the Crow. I take her clan as my main clan — Whistling Water. My kid clan is Piegan." Lani has twin brothers, Brandon "Buckskin" and Shannon "CP," who dance the Crow Traditional Straight Dance.

"It's a Crow tradition that you can't step over anybody," Julie explained. "You can't touch their face or hair unless they ask you to. You respect your father and brothers by not looking straight into their eyes or sitting next to them. And you can never, in traditional dancing, dance with your dad or brothers. You can dance with a cousin. When Lani gets older, she has to dance with her brother-in-law. Lani's Indian name is Sweetsage Woman. Her grandmother gave her that name in the Peyote meeting."

"My mother is my best friend. She's my role model, too. There are three main smells that Crow use in rituals and for praying — cedar, sweetsage, and bitter-root — and that is what my name is from. My grandmother

Dance fan

WISE WOMAN

AN OLD LADY SITS WAITING
FOR THE SONG TO BEGIN.

THE GRAY STREAKS IN HER HAIR
WEAVE IN AND OUT
OF HER LONG BRAIDS.

SHE WAS A WISE WOMAN
AND VERY PROUD OF ME.

SHE GETS UP SLOWLY, HELD DOWN
BY THE MANY YEARS SHE HAS SEEN.

SHE IS NOT JUST A MEMORY
OF MY GRANDMOTHER
SHE IS A MEMORY OF
A WISE WOMAN.

got the name Sweetsage Woman because sweetsage was the most important part of her praying in the Sun Dances and Tobacco Ceremonies and all aspects of her life, and at Peyote meetings to cleanse and purify. So she gave me the name Sweetsage Woman to carry on for her because she wouldn't be using the sweetsage anymore.

"I want to go to college and become an actress. I don't want to be stuck on the reservation with nothing to do, with only a high school degree. I want to move on with my life. I want to be somebody, not an anybody. I want to be a leader instead of a follower. I want to say no to drugs and tobacco.

"I'd like my people to respect their culture and their ways, to not drink or show up drunk or smoke too much. I want my people to understand that if they don't change, they'll lose their culture, they'll lose it all, and we have had it for thousands of years. And I want for my people to have pride in themselves instead of thinking they are not good because they are Indians. I want my people to understand the beauty that surrounds them and not take if for granted, to take care of Mother Earth. We owe so much to the land — we live off it. "

Gourd rattles

Acknowledgments

There are many people whom we wish to thank: R. C. and Bobbie and The Plainsmen for their hospitality in Montana, their friendship, and their help and guidance throughout the book; the Oglewanagi Gallery for allowing us to photograph many of the arts, crafts, and regalia in their gallery and for their help and guidance; Chipa Wolf for introducing us to the powwow circuit and, of course, Samson the bear for keeping us entertained and Thunder the buffalo for keeping us on our toes; Diamond Brown and his family for advice and continued friendship; Moakler Photographic Services for the processing and expert handling of all of our film and for their valued support; Color Chrome Atlanta for their generous support and quality Cibachromes; Russell Image Processing for their excellent black-and-white prints and support.

We would also like to thank the American College in Atlanta for their support in promoting the book; Michael Astalos for his enduring friendship and support; John Yow and all the people at Longstreet Press for believing in us; Barbara Dominey for her outstanding representation; and all of the dancers and craftspeople who gave so generously of their time. A very special thanks to each of our families and our friends for their loving support.